PAMELA GREEN is the mother of two sons, Sammie and Sawy, and a daughter Yasmeen. When her ex-husband abducted the three children in 1989, her long and arduous battle to regain custody of her children began. Five years on, she is as determined as ever to reunite her family and has offered help and advice to many other women in similar circumstances.

DEAR
CHILDREN

PAMELA GREEN
with Brigid McConville

PAN BOOKS
London, Sydney and Auckland

This edition published 1994 by Pan Books Ltd

a division of Pan Macmillan Publishers Limited
Cavaye Place London SW10 9PG
and Basingstoke

Associated companies throughout the world

ISBN 0 330 33264 3

A CIP catalogue record for this book is available from the
British Library

Typeset by Parker Typesetting Service, Leicester
Printed and bound in Great Britain by
Cox & Wyman Ltd, Reading, Berkshire

Acknowledgements

My book is dedicated to my father, Albert Green, who instilled in me a fierce determination to defend my rights and to achieve my aims. And to my sister Kath, without whose love, loyalty and support, I could not have made it through the past five years.

My thanks to Brigid McConville for helping me to write this book, to my sister Madaleine and my brother Dave, and to Catherine Hurley for her patience and professionalism.

For moral and practical support, my thanks go especially to: The British Ambassador to Egypt, Christopher Long, The Chairman of House of Frazer, Mr Mohammed Al-Fayed, Esther Rantzen, Anne Diamond, Jackie McKeown, Caroline Davies of *The Mail on Sunday*, Mary Riddell of *Today* newspaper, 'Uncle' Harry Arnold of the *Daily Mirror*, BBC News Room South-East (especially Cheryl Garnsey), Mike Mortimer of Carlton Television and Ian Austin of the *Croydon Advertiser*.

Thank you to the Rt Hon. Douglas Hurd; former British Vice-Consul, Helen Holmes; British Consul, Anita Sheldon; former British Ambassador to Egypt, Sir James Adams; British Pro-Consul, Youssef Fouad Youssef; and to Dame Angela Rumbold MP.

Thank you to my friends in Egypt: Farida Ghaly, Zeinab Abdel-Menaam, Mustapha Aheen and Nawaal Mustapha of *El-Akhbar* newspaper, Moataz Demerdash and all of the staff at Viz News and Video Cairo.

Thanks to my lawyer, Madam Madiha Luxour, with more respect and admiration than words can express; and thanks also to Dr Nabil Helmy and Miss Madeh Ahmed.

Special thanks to the medical team at Heliopolis Hospital in Cairo who saved my life: Dr Sammie Ramzy, Dr Ashraf Hammouda and Dr Samir Sultan.

Thank you, Officer Hatim El-Bibaany, for your honesty and dedication to your duty.

Thank you, Susy Jones, and thank you, Hedda Lyons.

Thank you to all of my friends and supporters who prefer to remain anonymous: Irene, AR, Diana, Mr Roberts, David Phillips . . .

My heartfelt thanks to my agent Peter Tauber, for his patience and unstinting confidence in me.

But most of all my thanks go to the British people who rallied to my side. I have not fought this battle alone.

Foreword by Anne Diamond

When I first met Pamela Green I couldn't help but feel extremely moved by her harrowing and heartbreaking account of her on-going struggle to re-unite with her children who were so heartlessly abducted by her ex-husband to his native Egypt.

Pamela's story is not just that of one mother's total devotion and love for her children, but sadly a story of our times. With thousands of similar cases every year, Pamela's incredible determination and indomitable spirit will not fail to leave a deep impression on the millions of women who have children as well as the many others who will become mothers in the future.

Anne Diamond

Prologue

Dear Children,

I keep missing you.

You are always in my dreams. Sometimes I hear your laughter like an echo of not so distant fun and happiness.

Sometimes, like a gift from God, my dreams are precious time spent with you. Sometimes my dreams allow me the pleasure of touching you and smelling the sweetness of your bodies and of your breath.

At home, your scooters have gone rusty but I've still kept them for you. They are too small for you now, but I can't bear the thought of throwing them away. Maybe you'll come back to me one day and maybe your scooters will bring back happy memories.

I've still kept your teddies, unwashed, so that any trace of your cuddles are not rinsed away.

I keep missing you. It hurts more every day. But you are always with me, even in my sleep.

Dear Sammie,

I still remember your soft, peachy cheeks on mine as I carried you, and I would hate it if the day ever came when I could not remember your soft rosebud lips whispering in my ears and kissing me on my mouth so gently.

Your teddy is wearing your grey duffle coat. The sleeves of the coat have taken the shape of your arms, and there are still sweetie wrappers in the pockets.

Sometimes I take the duffle coat off teddy so that I can see the shape that your arms made in your coat. And when I do I remember you, running ahead of me in the street, your arms slightly bent as you ran.

Dear darling Sawy,

Keep your secret thoughts and dreams. No one can take those away from you, my boy. I keep your toys that you loved: your farm animals, and especially the cow that you wouldn't allow out of your sight for too long.

Dear Sawy, do you remember how we used to call out 'goodnight' to each other – and then we would call 'Goodnight John-Boy', 'Goodnight Mary Ellen' – as if we were 'The Waltons'? Yasmeen and I still do that sometimes so as to remember the bedtimes which once led on to a peaceful night's sleep. There has been no peace without you and your brother, my darling.

I am sure that I get messages from you sometimes, and I always know when you are calling for me to come to you. I know when you are in trouble; I know when you are pining desperately for me. But I don't know where you are, darling. I haven't let you down; I just don't know where you are my love, they won't tell me.

Part One

Chapter One

'My name is Yasmeen. I am nine years old. I came to Cairo on holiday with my Daddy and my brothers. I was happy until Sammie ran out on to the balcony crying and said, "Daddy says we can't ever go home again because Mummy has gone crazy and she is in a mental hospital."

'I said "Don't tell lies", but my father came out and told me to shut up. I went to look for my brother Sawy and found him under the bed, crying. I didn't know how to comfort them; I was too confused myself.

'I wanted to escape using a ladder, but I told my stepmother and she told my father. We told Daddy that we wanted to speak to Mummy on the telephone, but he said, "If you go anywhere to ask for a telephone to call her, you'll be arrested."

'We went to see a man who asked us lots of questions [the Public Prosecutor]. Daddy told me if I didn't say what he told me to, he would beat me. But when the man asked me if I wanted to live in Egypt, I didn't answer. The boys came in later and said the opposite because they were scared of what Daddy would do to them.

'I had begged the man not to tell Daddy what I had said, but he must have, because when we got home Daddy slapped me until my head ached and locked me in the room without food for ten days. My brothers smuggled bread, water, cheese and tomatoes into my room at night, but even so I felt very strange and dizzy when I was allowed out.

'My grandfather was always hitting me and my brothers with a belt. I know that my brothers want to be with my mother, but they are scared that grandfather will hit them and spit in their faces again, as well as calling my mother dreadful names. I don't know why my grandfather would always follow me into the bathroom and stay standing there.

'Later my grandfather took me to the "doctor" to be circumcised, but I kicked and screamed until the doctor gave up.

'I was wondering – does my mother really love us? If she did, she would have come and taken us away from those terrible people!'

On the morning of Monday 10 December 1990, I woke up aching and exhausted in a ramshackle Cairo flat. I knew that no amount of sleep could restore me, and that there could be no peace for me until I held my children's small hands in mine. Not wanting to surface and face reality, I dragged myself to the kitchen to make tea that I didn't really want to drink.

My children's suffering was a constant torment to me in every waking and sleeping moment, and in my heart I felt that I too deserved no comfort, not even the comfort of morning tea. Memories of dreams of the children still clouded my head, but I knew that I must discipline myself and face the day, so I banished all thoughts of dreams and omens and forced myself towards the bathroom.

I stood above the drain that also functioned as a toilet and had my 'shower': this meant emptying pots and pans of cold water, gathered from a trickling tap, over my head. As the cold water shocked me awake, the significance of this day hit home. This was to be my last twenty-four hours that I would spend without my children, the last day of torturing myself with thoughts of their pain and suffering – thoughts which were almost too much to bear.

There was no time to waste. I quickly towelled myself dry and dressed in jeans and a T-shirt, thinking of all that I had to do to prepare for the rescue operation. I drank my tea sitting on the sofa that doubled as my bed in the living room.

For several months now – my money having run out – I had been staying with Sittee (meaning lady), which is what we called the grandmother of my Egyptian lawyer Medhat El-Zohiry. Sittee's home consisted of three separate, concrete rooms, each padlocked on the outside whenever she went out, which stood among pots of jasmine and washing lines on the roof of a six-storey block of flats.

I went over the notes that I had made the night before, though there was no real need. I knew all that I had to do by heart. I had to make last minute checks that everything – and everybody – was ready for dawn of the next day. Above all, I had to make certain that the men I was paying to help me were ready for their task of reclaiming my children.

For the most part of fourteen months I had been living here in the Abbassia District of Cairo. To begin with I had rented various flats in Abbassia, a colourful, bustling area of shops and markets sandwiched between downtown Cairo and the posher, outer suburbs. Abbassia had become my second home and the Arabic which I had learned in previous years had now become very fluent.

It was a tightly-knit community where everyone knew each other's business and, although I was the only European living there, I felt that I was accepted as a member of the community. Local people greeted me whenever I went out and kept a friendly eye on my welfare.

So far I had avoided harassment by respecting local customs and dressing carefully. And people who had seen the press reports of my case were mostly sympathetic. No doubt it also helped that my lawyer Medhat was a local boy made good. The fact that I was often in his company provided me, as a single woman, with essential protection in a Muslim society.

Medhat was the junior lawyer assigned to my custody case and he had worked for me since I flew to Cairo in September 1989 to get my children back after their abduction by my Egyptian ex-husband. Since then I had tried again and again to get justice through the processes of law.

In that terrible year I had longed to see my children, to hold them, to comfort them – and to tell them that they had been taken by their father against my will. I wanted them to know that I would stop at nothing to get them back.

Yet, in defiance of an order by the Public Prosecutor, my ex-husband had refused to let me see them. When I first went to Cairo after their abduction, three visits were arranged by lawyers. Each time I waited, holding carrier bags full of gifts for my children, but my husband never turned up.

On the third occasion – only hours before I was due to fly home to England – my ex-husband arrived alone. He told me and my lawyers that his father had forbidden him to bring the children to see 'their prostitute of a mother'.

My senior lawyer, Sayeed Al-Mahmoudy, seeing that I was distraught, managed to arrange a meeting for 8.30 that night in his office. And then he began to speculate: should we snatch the children back? Should we get some men to help us? It would be very expensive . . .

In the end he decided that a snatch would be bad for his reputation. Instead he told me to make my face look terrible, as if I had been crying, and to lie dramatically on the

6

sofa in his office as my ex-husband and children arrived.

I didn't want the children to see me looking distressed, but I did lie on the sofa – until I heard their footsteps in the hallway. The office was crowded: Medhat was there, along with other lawyers and servants in Al-Mahmoudy's employ and his mistress. My ex-husband and his lawyers milled around too. The room was full of smoke and jammed with curious onlookers, when all I wanted was a quiet visit with my children.

My son Sawy, aged seven, came into the room first. I could see his distress: he threw himself into my lap, both arms around my neck. Sammie, aged five, came towards me soundlessly mouthing 'Mummy', 'Mummy', and put his arms around me in a big bear hug. Then he whispered: 'Mum, I've got a secret. We're going to a new school and we're going to live in a new flat.'

My daughter Yasmeen, aged nine, stood by looking very tense and worried. She could see that my ex-husband was sitting near the door where he could hear every word. She knew her brothers would be punished for showing me affection: already she was protecting them, taking my place.

I flew home the day after the visit, 3 November, to begin campaigning and fundraising in England. I wanted to be as busy and productive as possible. I treated my campaign as a career, working as hard as I could and confining my feelings of desolation and loss to times when I could be alone.

I went back to Cairo in January only to hear that my case had been adjourned yet again. My lawyer told me then that my case would take not two or three months, as he had first predicted, but two or three years. I didn't know it at the time, but in charging a fee of £5,000 (sterling) he was exploiting me mercilessly. The fee should not have been more than £500 (sterling).

I went back to Cairo again in March, having sold our family furniture, begged and fundraised enough money to live there for some months. I rented a flat in Abbassia for £100 a month and filled it with flowers to cheer myself up.

In April 1990 came the devastating verdict that the Egyptian court would not recognize the English legal documents which gave me custody of my children. They would not recognize my divorce either. Helen Holmes, Vice-Consul at the British Embassy, broke the news to me as gently as possible but I fell apart. Seven months had been wasted waiting for this judgement; seven months in which my children had been beaten and abused.

Yet it was a turning point: I decided that I would have to rescue my children myself. My lawyer Medhat, knowing that custody cases often take years in Egypt, agreed to help me. I sat with him in one street café after another, ignoring the curious and critical stares of Egyptian men, as Medhat put the word out. I wanted it to be known among the kind of men who would risk a prison sentence that I was prepared to pay for their help.

Everywhere we went, Medhat – whose nickname in Egyptian was 'Silver Tongue' – carried my publicity file and talked about my case. One day we got a taxi and Medhat told my story to the driver, Mohammed. Mohammed said he knew just the person to help us. He introduced us to a man who claimed to have been a Brigadier in the Egyptian army. The 'Brigadier' agreed to recruit other men and to rescue my children. His price was £1200.

*

For much of the time the children had been living in their grandparents' two-roomed flat in the Sharabiya district, a notorious and dangerous ghetto which was a no-go area to local police and taxi drivers. Here Yasmeen, Sammie and Sawy had been living and playing among the rubbish, rats and cockroaches. I feared especially that, with his asthma, the dust and rubble of Sharabiya would damage Sammie's health.

Yasmeen described Sharabiya as 'a really horrible area where all dogs have diseases and the boys hit them with sticks. There's loads of dust and dirty sand there, and because it's so hot you get sweaty and the dust sticks to your skin. When I walked into my grandparents' apartment (it has no bathroom and the "shower" is a tap over the "toilet") I thought "Yuk!"'

British journalists who later tried to get into Sharabiya on the trail of my children at first met with refusal from their taxi driver who said it wasn't safe to go there. When they did persuade a driver to take them in, their vehicle was surrounded by menacing people and, alarmed, they made a quick retreat. They told me later that although they had been in the poorest areas of Calcutta, they had never seen a more shocking slum than this.

But my ex-husband later rented another flat in a quieter area called Gezr El-Suez, and the children were shunted between the two addresses. This was the new flat that Sammie had told me about in a whisper, and I found out where it was by dressing in borrowed Muslim clothes, waiting outside the school gates and secretly following the children home. (I did this on several occasions until I knew their routine, once sitting beside them on the bus but never able to make myself known to them for fear of jeopardizing my planned rescue attempt.)

In March 1990, knowing that my ex-husband and his parents had said dreadful things about me to the children (I was a 'prostitute', a 'drug addict', an 'alcoholic'), I resolved that I would go to Sharabiya by myself and see my children. The British Embassy warned me of the risks. They had already received an anonymous letter from a neighbour in Sharabiya warning that my ex-husband and his family were planning to kill me. Anybody could attack me, they said, and I was advised not to drink anything there in case I was poisoned.

But I *had* to see my children. At a time when I knew the grandfather would be at work (he was a big and violent man), I walked up to the flat and knocked on the door. The grandmother opened it. I quickly said, 'Mother, please will you let me see my children, I am a mother, the same as you,' and – completely against my inclination – I took and kissed her hand. I would have done anything to be with my children.

Through the door I could see Effet, the children's new stepmother, who looked astonished, and my Yasmeen. The grandmother let me in, but she was ranting at me – 'I can look after your children better than you' – and I was afraid she would call some men to attack me. Yet I managed to talk to my children and to tell them, don't worry, I am fighting for you. I could see that Yasmeen was under enormous pressure. She refused to sit next to me, fearing what punishment might follow.

I heard later in horrific detail how all the children were being beaten, slapped, spat at and abused. Yet as a girl in Egypt, Yasmeen was receiving worse treatment than the boys and her grandparents had plans to have her circumcised (a ritual removal of the clitoris intended to preserve virginity by suppressing sexual desire).

I talked to the children about school and about

homework; I wanted my visit to be as normal as possible. But when I hugged them the grandmother became furious that they showed affection for me, and I feared that they would be made to suffer for it.

In the summer of 1990, the 'Brigadier' and his team waited until the children's grandfather had gone out to work (my ex-husband had long since gone to America, leaving the children with his new wife Effet and his parents). Armed to the teeth with knives, the men went up to the flat.

They knocked at the door and told the grandmother that her husband had been taken ill at the bus-stop and that she must come down. Their plan was to get her to open the door a little, and then to burst in. I stood on the stairwell, out of sight.

The grandmother looked suspiciously through the door's spy hole, keeping the door on a chain. One of the team seemed to be high on drugs: these men commonly smoked hashish as well as injecting a drug called 'max', comparable to acid. When she saw them, the grandmother shouted 'Go away!', and slammed the door shut. I had to hurry down the stairwell, escaping under the balcony of the flat without being seen, not wanting the grandparents to know that I had discovered their address.

In October 1990, I tried again to rescue my children. This time I used a different team of men, again recruited by the taxi driver Mohammed, paying them £400. As we planned this new rescue attempt, one of the men told me a story about his sick child in hospital and asked me for some money on account. With the money I gave him he bought drugs and disappeared for days. I was learning not to part with my money too soon.

For the second rescue attempt, my sister Kath had flown

out from England to join me. We sat in a car outside the children's school playground, watching the children arrive. The plan was that when the grandfather had left them, the team of men were to go into the playground and bring the children out.

In the event, they simply lost their nerve. One of the team, known as The Fridge (he was 'so cold he could kill anybody'), thought he saw the grandfather returning, and he called out, 'There is the grandfather, run!' Terrified, the rest of the men fled from the playground.

Meanwhile, Yasmeen and Sammie were already outside the school gates with Medhat, who had told them he had a message for them. I could practically feel them on my lap, but Sawy was in the other playground and we couldn't get to him.

Kath was saying to me: 'You must wait for Sawy, you can't leave him on his own!' And then The Fridge and his men came running. Their flight alerted the caretaker; he grabbed Yasmeen and Sammie and quickly slammed the school gates shut with my children inside.

I was so ill with grief after that day that I felt every bone in my body might break. My weight had gone down to seven stone, my nerves were ragged and I looked like a walking skeleton. I tormented myself with regrets: if only I had taken the two children, I could have tried to rescue Sawy later. Then we could have been together again, and so much suffering could have been avoided.

By now I was becoming quite an old hand at recruiting shady Cairenes to help me – not a role that I had foreseen for myself when I lived an ordinary domestic life in Croydon. This, my third, rescue attempt was to be led by a man called Ahmed who had heard of my dilemma through the local grapevine. My fee for the job had gone down to £300: my funds were running dangerously low and I had been forced to abandon my flat and to move in with Sittee.

Ahmed was built like a bull and full of self-confidence. He was a natural leader, constantly surrounded by friends and followers, and he was not afraid to take the law into his own hands. I sensed also that he could be ruthless. I wouldn't want Ahmed to be my enemy, but I could certainly use his qualities as an ally. Ahmed recruited three men – Waheed, Ibrahim and Mohammed – from his formidable network of friends and former gaolbirds.

On this particular Monday morning, before my third snatch attempt, my first task was to make sure that none of the team had gone missing or had committed crimes overnight, landing themselves in prison again.

Before I left Sittee's flat I looked into the mirror, scraping my hair back into a pony-tail. I looked terrible: my eyes were dull and ringed with dark circles. I had been unable to eat properly for months and looked anorexic. But my looks no longer mattered to me. There was only one thought on my mind and it drove me on relentlessly: how to get my children back?

I climbed down the dilapidated spiral staircase, its wrought iron balustrade barely held together with scraps of electrical wire, to the street below. Then I forced myself to stride purposefully towards the rickety sandwich stall where Ahmed eked out his living.

As I passed through the street market towards Ahmed's stall the market traders greeted me cheerily: 'Ezzayek ya Um Yasmeen!' I was very proud of my title: 'Um Yasmeen' means mother of Yasmeen and I knew that it was a sign of respect and a term of endearment among Egyptian people.

But little did my local friends know that I had a secret plan for the next morning, and little did they know of the worries which plagued me on that day:

What if the men let me down in the morning?

What if Ahmed hadn't yet come back from Port Said where he had gone to conclude an illegal deal?

What if there weren't enough seats on the British Airways flight to take my children home tomorrow?

But 'what-ifs' weren't going to do me or the children any good. I knew that I had to do everything methodically, eliminating all the tasks on my list one by one.

I crossed the tramlines in the middle of the busy main road and quickened my steps towards Ahmed's stall. He wasn't there. I felt panic rising inside me. Was today going to be yet another day of despair and sadness? Ahmed had promised me that he would return from Port Said to Cairo by 9.00 that morning, and now it was 10.30.

I ran around the corner to our usual meeting place in the open air café, but he wasn't there either. I searched for his face in the crowds at the bus station, but there was no sign of him. Then I ran half the length of busy Abbassia street, dodging in and out between the taxis, buses and market stalls, until I reached the home of my lawyer Medhat.

Medhat's mother told me that he was in court and reminded me that I had arranged to meet him in the court-house at midday. I had almost forgotten that the verdict in my custody case was expected that day. The legal proceedings had become almost irrelevant as I concentrated all my energies on the plan to save my children. My throat was dry from running and from the panic that threatened to overwhelm me. I had to take control of myself. I stopped in the street and took deep, controlled breaths. I had so many things yet to do:

I had to buy the traditional Muslim headwear that would disguise me during the snatch operation.

I had to meet Medhat at the local Imbaba courthouse at midday.

I had to get to the British Embassy before one o'clock to speak to the Vice-Consul Helen Holmes.

I had to confirm four seats on the British Airways flight to London for the next morning.

Most important of all, I had to keep calm.

I fixed my mind on my aim. Twenty-four hours to go and I had to be successful in recovering my dear children. Now was the time for me to draw on all my inner strength. I needed my last reserves of energy and determination. I would complete the tasks I had set myself – and then I would go back and look for Ahmed.

I hailed a passing taxi, calling out my destination: El-Hussein. And just as the taxi pulled up beside me, Ahmed's right-hand man Waheed appeared out of the crowd in the street saying, 'Good morning. Where have you been?'

I was so relieved to see him that the words tumbled out of my mouth: 'Waheed! I'm so glad to see you! Where have *you* been? And *where* is Ahmed?'

Waheed told me that Ahmed had arrived back from Port Said early that morning and had gone straight to the street in Gezr El-Suez where my children were staying. Ahmed had been checking that the children were still there, and he had seen my little Sammie on the balcony of the flat. He reassured me that Ahmed would be back in Abbassia by midday, but as I had to be in court at that time I left a message for Ahmed: 'Tell Ahmed that Medhat and I will meet him at 3.30 this afternoon at the usual café. And tell him that it is tomorrow – or never!'

Waheed knew from my tone that I was deadly serious and he promised faithfully to pass the message on. I shook hands with him and got into the taxi.

On the drive to El-Hussein I stared out of the window at the streets of Cairo, congested with traffic and teeming with people. Three times in recent months I had been on the verge of rescuing my children with this team, but each time my hopes had been dashed at the last moment. Each time something had gone wrong. Either one of the men could not be found, or Ahmed had announced in an important voice that 'it won't be successful today'.

The last time had been only a few days ago. We had waited in a car near the children's address in El Sharabiya. Ahmed and Waheed had leapt out of the car, high on adrenalin. Those minutes had seemed like years to me. Years of holding myself back from jumping out of the car after Ahmed so that I could sweep my babies up into the safety of my arms. Minutes that felt like years of forcing myself to heed the words of Medhat and the other men as they said 'Wait! Not now! Hold yourself until the signal!' Minutes and years of torture that ended in . . . nothing.

Ahmed came back and said: 'It's too busy here, we'll get murdered by local men if there is any trouble. We'll have to do it from the other flat.'

I had watched helplessly as my children dragged themselves past the car where I sat, their shoulders bowed under the weight of heavy school bags. The boys' heads had been shaved and they looked beaten; what had happened to the laughing, joyful children who had lived with me in Mitcham only a year before? They walked over the rotten rubbish of a fruit and vegetable market and then through a hole in a wall to cross train tracks. I saw what danger they risked and could only watch as they boarded a filthy, overcrowded tram on their way to school – and disappeared out of my sight.

I had no intention of allowing that to happen again. I had to get it right this time. I had a secret plan that I had revealed to no one. If the gang changed their minds or lost their courage at the last second, I would dash out of the car to save my children alone. I knew it meant risking my life; the grandfather was a strong and violent man. But he had been beating my children, and that was mental torture to me.

I no longer cared about my own safety. I only knew that I had to save my children from the cruelty of their life in Cairo and the violence of their grandfather, at any cost. Life without my beautiful children was going to be the death of me anyway. I would rather die than live without them. How I longed for the security of our organized, routine days together in England.

I was brought back to reality by the voice of the taxi driver asking me where I wanted to be dropped in the El-Hussein area. I paid off the taxi driver and within minutes I had found the shop that I needed. The sight of a European woman in a shop that specialized in strict Muslim women's clothing raised a few eyebrows. But I didn't waste any time in conversation with curious local people. I knew what I needed and within minutes I had bought the headscarves and had hailed another taxi.

As I directed the driver through the busy, winding streets towards the courthouse in the Imbaba district I prepared myself for the bad news that I was sure to receive there. I knew there would be yet another excuse, yet another delay. I would be given some date in the future, dangled in front of my nose like a carrot.

My case had been before the courts for fourteen months and there had been at least a dozen adjournments. I no longer held any hope in my heart of winning the custody battle in court. These legal proceedings were a sham but I had to be seen to be trying to go through the proper channels. No one would be able to say that I hadn't tried my best to win my children back within the law. And for as long as I struggled diligently with the red tape of the legal system, no one could accuse me of taking the law into my own hands.

I cheered myself with the thought that this would be the last time that I would have to face the stares of the curious at the courthouse. The last time that I would have to listen to the hypocrisy of the court officials who constantly implored me to have faith in God, Egyptian law and the presiding judge – while whispering in my ear that they needed more money, more bribes.

Who could blame me for planning drastic action?

Chapter Two

I took the winding staircase two steps at a time until I reached the second floor of the courthouse. I was anxious to get the formalities over with and to get on with the real business of saving my children. As I walked into the court writer's office everyone, as usual, jumped up to greet me: 'Ahlan! Ahlan!' (Welcome! Welcome!) The women workers gave me hugs and kisses; the men shook me warmly by the hand. But I didn't have time today to sit and chat with them so I got straight to the point and asked what had happened.

I knew the answer before they told me. It was written all over the face of Medhat who was sitting in the corner drinking tea with Mohammed Salama, the court writer. Mohammed came and spoke gently to me: 'God willing, God willing, God willing . . . the verdict will be next week. Never mind and don't worry. Keep your faith and you will get your rights because God is with you.'

The excuse this time was that Judge Saad Zelhoum was very ill in hospital. He was therefore unable to make a decision on my case. No other judge would rule on my case not knowing anything of the background. Even though I had known in my heart that my rights would not be restored to me that day, I couldn't help feeling angry and frustrated.

Through the open window of the court office I could hear the sound of children squealing with joy in the play-ground of the school next to the courthouse. Words of comfort were being showered on me by the court officials, but I couldn't take them in. All I could hear was the sweet sound of children at play. It struck me that although the children in that school playground were all calling to each other in Arabic, there was no difference between the sounds they made and the sounds of children playing in a primary school back home. My children once played like that in an English playground, rolling over each other like puppies.

The court workers wanted me to sit and drink tea with them, but I made my excuses to them and spoke to Medhat in English so that the others could not understand: 'Let's go. Ahmed is back from Port Said and we have got to meet him at 3.30 in the café.'

I didn't like the look on Medhat's face. I could see that he was nervous. Was he having second thoughts? I couldn't risk losing Medhat's support at this stage. I needed him to deal with Ahmed and his men. Without a male ally to stand up for me I would be very vulnerable and I knew that the gang would try to take advantage of my position as a woman.

We left the court and made our way to the British Airways office in Tahrir Square where I booked four seats on the 7.30 a.m. flight to Heathrow. And while we were in central Cairo I went over to see Helen Holmes, Vice-Consul at the British Embassy and my good friend and ally. Helen had been posted to Egypt in the same week that I had arrived to begin the battle for my children. She was a very warm and sympathetic person, as well as being decisive and full of life, and she had helped me through some of my darkest moments. We walked the short distance to her office arm in arm as she fussed over me like a mother: 'All right? Everything OK? You look very tired, Pam.' I tried to put her mind at rest: 'I'll be fine, don't worry about me. I just need a few weeks in the Bahamas.'

Helen always found time for me, no matter what. And like me, she was direct and determined. A colleague of Helen's once joked: 'You don't need the SAS to get your children back; you've got Helen Holmes in Cairo!'

Helen offered me a coffee in her office, but I explained that Medhat was waiting downstairs in the gatehouse. I needed Helen to know that I might need Embassy assistance the next day, but I had to be careful how I worded my warning. Although we had built up a close friendship, I had to remember Helen's position as a British diplomat. There were certain things that were best left unsaid between us.

'Helen?'

'Ye-es? What is it?'

'Helen, um, I'm going to be very busy early tomorrow. What time do you leave for work in the morning?'

She eyed me in a curious, amused way, but I knew better than to tell her any more. 'Well, Helen, it's just that I may very well need to speak to you urgently between six and seven tomorrow morning. And if I do need to speak to you, where can I contact you?'

She replied with mock sternness in her voice: 'Just phone the Embassy, girl! They'll put you through to me.'

Helen may or may not have guessed what I was about to do the next day, but now I knew that she would alert the Embassy security staff to be ready, should I call them for assistance.

I had to go; no time for jokes and coffee today. Helen hugged me warmly and told me to take care. And then I was off again, running down the stairs to join Medhat. We hurried out on to the street and hailed a taxi back to Abbassia. The traffic was terrible with cars bumper to bumper and drivers fighting for every inch, blaring their horns with irritation. By the time we arrived in Abbassia, both Medhat and I had terrible headaches. There was time for a break before our meeting with Ahmed, and so Medhat invited me to pay a visit to his mother, Farida.

Farida had been a source of comfort and inspiration to me for a long time, and I had grown to love and respect her. I knew that she would make a great fuss over me and I felt I needed a little pampering. Medhat's house was always busy – he had many brothers and sisters – but today Medhat's mother knew that I needed to sit alone with her and she shooed all of her children out of the house.

Medhat took the opportunity to tell me of his worries. How would it effect his career as a lawyer, if it was discovered that he had been involved in a snatch-back operation? I was not breaking the law by taking my children: legally, they belonged to me as much as to their father. But the men who helped me could be accused of child abduction, a crime which carries a prison şentence in Egypt.

'I cannot show my face tomorrow,' said Medhat. 'No one must see me. I will come with you and I will be there – but not at the moment at which you take your children.'

I knew that he had to protect himself, but I didn't want the four men of my team to know that he was not going to be directly involved. We devised a plan: Medhat would come with us in the car in the morning, but he would stand back from the snatch at the last moment.

Medhat's mother brought food for us, but I had had no appetite for months. She fed me like a baby, scolding me for not taking care of myself: 'Who will take care of your children if you are ill?' She knew of our plan for the next day but did not discuss it with us. It was as though talking about it would jeopardize our chances of success. But her eyes spoke volumes: I knew that she felt deeply for me, as one mother for another. We both knew that tomorrow would be make or break.

Before I left her house she hugged me tightly. We were both close to tears as she said simply, 'God go with you.'

Medhat and I walked slowly down Abbassia Street, each lost in our own thoughts, each of us weighed down under the heavy pressure of our separate worries for the next day.

Ahmed and Waheed were both waiting for us at the café, but they did not look happy. Ahmed said, 'There is no one home at the flat in Gezr El-Suez.' I flatly refused to believe him. My fears that the men would back out at the last moment were going to be realized if I didn't take control of the situation.

'Ahmed,' I said, in a very determined voice, 'I am not waiting any longer and I'm not coming up with any more masareef [expenses] on account.' (I had already given the men many small sums of money.) I insisted that we all went to check on the address, together and immediately, telling Ahmed that if he wasn't prepared to do the job the next day then I would find other men to help me. I took out the £200 that I had ready in my bag to pay him after we had rescued the children – and I waved it in his face.

'Put it away!' he said to me, 'someone will see you!'

But I had jolted him into action and Medhat and I, Ahmed and Waheed all set off for the half-hour car journey through heavy traffic to Gezr El-Suez. I covered my head with the disguise that I had bought earlier that day. The last thing I needed was for anyone to recognize me in the vicinity of the children's new address.

We parked the car in a side road and Ahmed told me to

stay in the car while he checked. But I wanted to see with my own eyes and I was so insistent that Ahmed had to agree.

Gezr El-Suez is a mixed district of flats and shops with a six-lane road running through its centre. On one side of the road is the five-star El-Salam hotel where British Airways crew often stay while in Cairo. On the other side is a jumble of five-storey flats set among sandy, unpaved streets. The children were staying with their grandparents in one of these flats: my ex-husband was still in America.

I walked down the street near to the El-Salam Hotel and stood at the bus-stop, pretending to wait for a bus. From there I had a clear view of the balconies at the front of the flats. I didn't have to wait long before I saw movement on the balcony of the children's flat. It was the grandmother hanging out washing – and who was with her but Sawy! My heart skipped a beat with excitement.

I didn't wait to see the other children: if Sawy was there I knew they'd all be there. I wanted to run back to the car, but forced myself to walk at a normal pace. Back in the car there was no need for me to tell the news; it was written all over my face. I was so happy I cried with joy.

They are there – and tomorrow they will be with me!

Ahmed said 'Mabrouk ya Um Yasmeen!' (Congratulations mother of Yasmeen) and then, 'Tomorrow, OK?'

Ahmed and Waheed were hungry so we set off to eat in a restaurant in Abbassia as a kind of celebration. I was glad of the chance to sit with the men and go over their plan. We needed a last conference before the rescue. We went via the back streets of Abbassia to pick up Mohammed, the driver, and Ibrahim, the fourth member of the team.

While I waited in the car in the narrow, winding streets, young children came to me to practise their elementary

English: 'Hello! I love you!' they said. I was happy to laugh and joke with them, enjoying every moment of talking with children again, holding my secret close in my heart . . .

Soon I'll be chatting with my own children. __

And then, all assembled in the busy, noisy restaurant, we sat in the corner so that nobody could overhear our conversation. Ahmed repeated the words that he had used time and time again: 'Any child that does not want to come, I will not take.' And, 'I will not use violence on the grandfather. He is old and we know that he has a bad heart.'

But I had no intention that anyone should use violence. The men would be carrying no weapons; at most they may have to restrain the grandfather. And I had no doubt that the children desperately needed to be with their mother.

Only days before, Yasmeen had begged me to take her and the boys away as soon as possible. I had been to see them at the flat in Sharabiya – one of the half dozen visits that I had grudgingly been allowed to make in recent months (I would often arrive to an empty flat and be forced to wait another week).

Yasmeen had been waiting for me on the balcony and she risked a beating from her grandparents by sitting beside me and writing me a note in front of them. I whispered to her: 'Be careful: you will get into trouble.' But she was defiant. 'I don't care,' she whispered back. Her note begged me to save her without delay.

As Yasmeen told journalists later, she and the boys were being regularly beaten and humiliated, and their grandfather had been exposing himself to them: 'I really hated living with them. I had to do horrible jobs for my grandfather like cleaning his feet every day. My Uncle Gamal (Yasmeen's father's brother) used to beat us with this long pipe like a hosepipe, which really hurt but didn't leave any marks. It was so awful I don't like to talk or even think about it.'

But Yasmeen's desperation was fired with a new sense of urgency: only days before, her grandparents had tried to have her circumcised. She had overheard them talking about their plans and had refused to cooperate with the 'doctor'. She later said: 'I played dumb and pretended not to understand the "doctor". He told me to lie down. I refused and we had an argument. My grandfather tried to push me down and I kicked him in the chest. Then he chased me round the room – like cat and dog. Finally, my grandmother forced me on to the sofa. The "doctor" took a needle and started putting stuff into it.

'I was screaming my head off and kicking out all over the place. Luckily I managed to knock the needle out of the "doctor's" hand and it broke on the table. After this the "doctor" refused to continue with the operation. My grandfather sat spitting and swearing at me.'

Fearing that they would try again to circumcise her, Yasmeen's note pleaded with me to rescue her and Sammie and Sawy as soon as I could. I had vowed not to let her down, that I would come for her as soon as I could – but that she must not tell her brothers. I was afraid that, being so young, they would let the secret slip to their grand-parents or stepmother.

Ahmed and I went over the plan step by step, making sure that each man knew his part. Ahmed was to restrain the grandfather. Ibrahim and Waheed were to help me put the children in the waiting car. Mohammed the driver was only to step in if absolutely necessary. Otherwise he was to wait in the car and to keep the engine running.

Ahmed then wanted a private word with me. I knew what was coming: taking advantage of the fact that I was

26

excited and happy, he asked me for expenses on account. But I knew better than to agree. From past, bitter experience I knew exactly what they would do with the money. They would go out and buy hashish to smoke through the night and then they would be useless the next morning.

I told Ahmed that he could have all of the rest of the money the next morning when the children were with me, but not a moment before. He wasn't happy and he tried hard to persuade me, but in the end he agreed to my conditions.

Then I shook hands with the men and made my way to Sittee's flat to rest for a few hours. Sittee was at home and glad of my company. I knew that it would be impossible for me to sleep, so I was glad of her company too. As usual, she regaled me with all the latest gossip on the community in Abbassia; who had died, who had been married and who looked likely for divorce. It was good therapy for me to listen to this sweet old woman telling me of other people's plight, and it took my mind off my immediate dilemma, if only for a few hours.

But I couldn't possibly confide in her about the plan for tomorrow: the news would be all over Abbassia if I did. So I was forced to feign calm behaviour, and after a while I began to feel calmer.

Sittee took pride in the fact that although she was over eighty years old, she could still fuss over guests in her humble, poverty-stricken home. She insisted on making tea for me, and I knew that to try to stop her would make her feel her age and would offend her. We drank our tea together, happy that we were sharing each other's company, and happy that we felt like sisters despite the difference in our ages. We discussed life in general and secretly confided in each other that most men were absolutely despicable!

Medhat came to see me at about nine that evening. He looked terrible and I knew that he was still worrying about the implications of the rescue attempt for his career. 'Medhat,' I said to him, 'if you want to pull out I will understand and I will not be disappointed in you.' But his fighting spirit returned and he said, 'No, I cannot. The men will let you down if I'm not there.'

He suggested we join the men in the café on the Square to make sure that they were all still together. We went down the dark, winding staircase, Medhat lighting the way with matches, until we reached the street. The market there was still buzzing, the stalls lit by kerosene lamps, and the atmosphere was one of jolly camaraderie. It had been raining and the poorly constructed road was slippery with mud. As we weaved our way through the market stalls, trying to avoid huge puddles, friends called to us to join them for tea, coffee, or just a chat.

But we pressed on until we reached the café and found the men sitting together, playing Towla (backgammon). They welcomed us to the table, and even in the midst of the pressure that was on us all, we still managed to pass the occasional joke and laugh with each other. No onlooker would have guessed our secret plan.

Ahmed leaned over and said to me 'Mabrouk!' (congratulations!) in anticipation of success less than eight hours away. My face lit up. I had done all that I possibly could in preparation: the rest was up to God.

Medhat and Ahmed tried to persuade me to go home and rest, but I didn't want to be alone. I stayed with them until just after 11 o'clock, and then I made my way back to Sittee's house. In the tiny living room that doubled as my bedroom, I longed to be able to fall into a deep sleep and then to wake refreshed, but my mind would not relax. Instead, I sat chain-smoking and wishing that the long, dark hours would pass faster. I imagined myself in every possible situation the next morning . . .

Ordering Yasmeen into the car.

Picking up little Sammie boy.

Urging Sawy to run faster.

I needed to do something with my hands, so I checked that my clothes were ready for the morning and set them out on the chair by my bed: a flowery, long-sleeved blouse; a maxi-length skirt to be worn over jeans; the long, flowing Muslim headwear.

I planned to slip out of the skirt and headwear as soon as the children were safely with me. That way we would look like any other European family on holiday in Egypt. I knew the children would be wearing their school uniforms when we picked them up. That would look suspicious at the airport – only twenty minutes' drive from the flat – so I had packed new clothes for them to change into in the car.

I had chosen typical tourist wear for the children: there were jeans from London and T-shirts from Cairo's Khan El-Khalil tourist bazaar. Sawy's T-shirt sported a comical-looking camel standing beside the Pyramids, and Sammie's T-shirt was gaily printed with hieroglyphics. Yasmeen's had the logo 'I LOVE EGYPT'. I had also packed other clothes for the children in my suitcase just in case we were searched at the airport, to make everything look completely normal.

I knew that even at the last moment I could be stopped from taking my children out of the country. Egypt's security services keep tabs on all its citizens, and Egypt has been technically in a 'state of emergency' for many years. Every person trying to leave or enter the country is logged on to computer, and if my ex-husband had taken legal steps to stop me taking my children home, we would not get past passport control.

I had even heard tell of a British woman journalist married to an Egyptian whose husband had taken her and their two sons to the airport for a trip to Europe: she was stopped from boarding her plane because she didn't have his permission to leave the country, and she had to run back to the car park and obtain his signature before she was allowed to travel.

But I had done what I could to anticipate any problems at the airport. Through contacts of mine I had bribed immigration officers at Cairo airport to check and double check their computers. There was nothing on those computers to stop me from leaving the country with my children. If all went well we would be on the 7.30 a.m. flight to London.

3.10 a.m. Two hours to go. Every second bringing me closer to our reunion. Medhat arrived at Sittee's flat again, his face lined with fatigue and worry. I asked him if everything was OK. He said: 'Yes, no problem. We will meet the men by the bus station at 5.15. But remember what I told you: don't pay Ahmed until the children are in the car with you.'

We drank more tea. We smoked more cigarettes. My head was throbbing with pain and my ears were full of ringing noises.

4.30 a.m. Time to get dressed. I washed my face with icy

cold water and changed into the clothes that I had set out. All dressed and ready. I sat quietly for a while and prayed:

Please God, stay with me.

Please God, help my children and me.

Please God, stay with me.

Chapter Three

5.00 a.m. Sittee is sleeping soundly. I kiss her very gently and then Medhat and I leave in complete silence.

I am going down the stairs. It is happening now. I have waited for so long, and it is happening now.

Even at this time of the morning there are people about. The owner of the juice bar is hosing the floor clean. The newspaper stand on the corner is open for business. Young men are gathered around an all-night fruit stall.

In the street Medhat and I walk apart from each other for his protection. No one must know of his involvement in the plan.

My children must be awake now, and getting ready for school.

The Peugeot Estate with its three tiers of seats pulls up just as I approach the bus station. Mohammed is driving and Ahmed is seated next to him. Ibrahim and Waheed are sitting together behind. I climb into the very back seat, saying the traditional Muslim greeting 'Assalamu Ala-ykum' (Peace be upon you). Everyone replies 'Salam. Ou Rahma T allah' (And the kindness of God upon you).

Medhat is further down the street, waiting for us to pick him up. Before we drive the short distance, Ahmed says: 'Medhat is not going to be any help. He is too nervous.'

'Yes, I know,' I say. 'But still he must come with us.'

Medhat climbs in and we set off. I check my watch: 5.15 exactly. We're on time. It is pitch black and we are all silent. I have pains in my stomach. The men are all chain-smoking: the tension is obvious and still building. It is all too much for poor Medhat. He orders Mohammed to stop the car, quickly! He vomits in the street; his nerves have got the better of him.

I hope he doesn't make the others too nervous.

Back on the road again, Ahmed says: 'I'm not going to do it today if the children's stepmother takes them to school. I'm not in the business of frightening women.'

You dare let me down, Ahmed!

Ahead I can see the El-Salam Hotel.

We are here. My children are here.

We drive past the El-Salam and then back on ourselves, turning right into the slip road that leads to the street where the children live. Medhat gets out of the car to wait near the bus-stop on the main road.

Please God, stay with me. Please God, don't leave me.

There is a man selling breakfast sandwiches on the corner of Mecca Street, so we park the car further away, not wanting to raise suspicions.

Ahmed sends Mohammed off to walk past the children's flat and to check that there is nobody around to get in our way. He is gone for six full minutes and I can hardly breathe: 'Ahmed! Where is he? What if the children come down now, when we have no driver?' Ahmed reassures me: 'Don't worry, it is still too early.'

Mohammed returns and tells us: 'The balcony is already

open and there are two children leaning over and looking down.'

I'm here for you children; I'm waiting for you darlings.

I don't feel nervous now; just determined that this time I will be successful in rescuing my children. I listen carefully to the men's hushed whispers, hoping and praying that none of them will lose their cool and let me down at the last minute.

It has to be today. I can't stand any more. I'm going to die soon if I don't get them back.

My entire being is on red alert. Unable to sit still I open and close my hands, open and close, open and close. I am grateful for the freedom that the Muslim headwear gives me to look around at the people walking in the street on their way to work. I am waiting for the first sight of my children as they make their way to the bus-stop for their long journey to school. Emotions suppressed, I wait like a coiled spring, ready for action.

Six o'clock. They'll be coming any minute now. On Ahmed's instructions, Mohammed drives the car to the other end of Mecca Street, closer to the children's flat.

Stay with me God.

I train my eyes on the entrance of the building. I don't even want to blink in case I miss the first fraction of a second when the children appear. And then suddenly I see them . . .

Yasmeena!

Yasmeen is the first to walk into the street, peering around her, scanning the area. And there is the grandfather. Then Sammie and Sawy appear.

34

'Go!', my brain orders me, 'Go! Now!' I say, 'Yela Ya Ahmed! There they are. Let's go!'

He turns in his seat and speaks to me, his tone firm and even: 'Give me the money. The men refuse to do the job without the money first.'

My eyes are locked on my children walking in the street just yards away from me. He has planned it well. I cannot argue. I hand him the money, simultaneously ordering Mohammed to drive towards my children: 'Slowly and carefully Mohammed, drive up behind them.'

Sammie and Sawy are holding hands. The grandfather is holding Yasmeen's hand. I open the car door slightly. I am poised, ready to jump. But as the car draws slowly next to my children, Sammie turns to look: he doesn't recognize me in the Muslim headwear.

The car slows in front of the grandfather and children. I fly out of the car and shout at my daughter: 'Yasmeen! Get in the car!' She panics momentarily and then makes a dash for the car.

My God. My boys are running away from me. My sons are screaming in terror.

Sawy runs back up the street, but Sammie's little legs carry him as fast as he can go in the *opposite* direction.

Who do I run after first?

Sammie is running towards the car and the men, so I lift my skirts and run like hell after Sawy, calling out to him, 'Sawy, it's Mama, it's Mama . . .' But he is terrified and as he runs he is screaming. The boys don't know I am coming to rescue them; they don't recognize me. Sawy dashes inside the entrance of a dark, gloomy block of flats. I pause, turn to see where Sammie is before I go in.

My God, I can't see the men or the car or Sammie, and the grandfather is striding towards me, his face savage with anger.

He pulls a knife from his right-hand trouser pocket and says 'Right, I am going to kill you now.' I see the knife coming. The blade is at least six inches long and curved like a sabre.

I'm trapped. I've got no chance.

I back away from him into the wall. In that split second I try to prepare for the pain, calling on the strength of my mind to receive it. He pounces forward and stabs me with all the force of his anger, low down and on my right side.

I feel no pain. I do not scream.

He butchers my abdomen mercilessly and with precision, thrusting the knife into my left side and ripping through my flesh to the right.

I'm going to die.

My abdomen feels strangely warm. It is my warm blood, pouring out of me. He hasn't finished yet. I grip his shoulder to stop myself from falling. My hands are covered in my own blood. I can see over his right shoulder. There are three men standing on the other side of the road, eating sandwiches. One is wearing a red quilted jacket. He looks over his shoulder at me and then turns away, unconcerned.

I plead with the grandfather: 'Bas! Kifayer. Bas!' (Stop. Enough. Stop.) He isn't going to stop. He pushes me away from him and stabs me in the middle of my chest. I fall to the floor. He leans over me and gouges the knife violently into my left breast, twisting and twisting, searching for my heart.

He puts his knee on the hilt of the knife and leans his whole body weight on to the weapon. I feel his breath on my face. I can smell him: he smells of evil.

Suddenly, he stops and is gone. I haven't screamed once.

He'll come back. He'll finish me off.

I have to get up. I have to put one foot in front of the other. I must get across the road to the El-Salam Hotel. I am weak but I am still alive. I still have a chance of saving myself. I am not going to end my life lying on a dirty Cairo street, not knowing what has happened to my children. I drag myself to my feet, and holding the largest wound together with my hands, I start walking.

My blood gushes from me as I drag myself to a standing position. I begin to walk, but the faster I walk, the faster the blood pours.

Walk steadily. You can make it.

My feet squelch in the blood that has rivered down my legs and into my shoes.

Please God, don't leave me.

I reach the main road and face the busy, six-lane carriageway, divided by a grassy central reserve. Cars swerve around me as I stagger across the lanes of traffic, one hand gripping my abdomen, the other raised up high to try to stop the oncoming cars.

When I reach the central reserve, I scan the streets looking for Medhat, the men and my children. But there is still no sign of any of them.

Keep on going. Don't stop walking.

I get to the other side of the road and lean against the high brick wall that surrounds the El-Salam Hotel. There is a man walking towards me and I beg him in Arabic: 'Please help me, I'm dying.' He runs off, terrified.

I hope the men have picked up the boys.

With each step, my body is growing weaker, but my determination to live is growing stronger.

Must get to the hotel. Must speak to the Embassy. Must tell who did this to me.

I stagger inside the main gate of the hotel and there is a man sitting in a small wooden hut, a telephone next to him. I speak to him, trying to modify my voice so as not to panic him: 'Please help me. I'm English and I've been stabbed. I'm dying. I must use your phone to call the British Embassy.'

He tells me that the phone isn't working, but I don't believe him and I pick it up: it is dead. I make him help me walk the rest of the way to the lobby.

I'll bleed on their carpets and then they'll help me.

My entire being has altered in state and I dip into a potent reserve of energy that I never knew I possessed. The automatic door to the lobby opens, and just inside are uniformed hotel staff. I notice that they are all wearing name badges and that one of the badges reads 'Manager'.

I speak to the Manager: 'I have been stabbed with a knife by my children's grandfather. I must speak to the British Embassy. I need a doctor.'

The hotel staff stand there, looking at me. I see the

38

telephone behind the concierge desk. It is my lifeline; I walk behind the desk and reach for the receiver. Before my hand reaches it, someone hurriedly throws a tissue over the receiver to stop my blood from dripping on it.

'How do I get a line?' I ask. 'Just dial nine,' comes the reply. They are going to let *me* do it. I know the Embassy number by heart and I get through straight away. Within seconds I am talking to Helen: 'Helen. It's Pam. I've been stabbed. The grandfather has stabbed me.'

She makes no reply. Perhaps she hasn't heard me. 'Helen. It's me. I've been stabbed.'

I hear her voice at last: 'Pam. Where are you?' She seems so far away. I wish that she were standing right next to me.

Helen will take care of everything now.

And for the first time since I had been stabbed I feel excruciating pain. I feel my lips tingle curiously, feel my energy draining out of me, feel myself becoming light.

I look to my right and see the gracious hotel staircase: how I wish that I were gliding down it in a ball gown . . .

My mind is wandering. I must stay conscious.

I am still holding the phone in my hand. The manager is agitated; it isn't good for business to have me standing there, dripping blood. Just before I pass out, I replace the receiver.

I have put the phone down and cut off my lifeline – without telling Helen where I am.

I surfaced briefly and knew that I was being carried. Then, someone was slapping my face, trying to revive me. I opened my eyes to find that I was lying on my back in another wooden hut. A man in uniform crouched on his knees beside me.

I assumed that he was a policeman. 'I need a doctor, not a policeman,' I said.

'Show me what has happened to you,' he said. I was afraid to show my body to him. He said (untruthfully), 'I am a doctor, not a policeman. Show me.'

I pulled up my blouse and saw the shock in his eyes. The colour drained from his face and he put his hand to his mouth. When he next spoke, his voice was angry: 'Who did this to you?'

'It was my children's grandfather,' I told him. 'His name is Mohammed El-Sawy.'

Then I said to him: 'You're not a doctor, are you?'

'No, I'm not,' he said. 'I'm a policeman. You must tell me everything: is he Egyptian?'

I fought to stay conscious in order to answer him: 'He lives just over the road at number 10 Mecca Street, and he also has another address – number 5 Hussein Mahmoud Street, Esbit-Belal – in Sharabiya. I was married to his son and his son kidnapped my children. I have a custody case in court, but it is taking too long. I tried to take my children back and the grandfather tried to kill me.'

I carried on talking, my mind working clearly while my body grew weaker: 'I had to try to take my children because I love them so much and they need me. After their father stole them from me, he left them with his parents, without their own mother or father.'

I had to get the policeman's sympathy: I was the victim of attempted murder, but I was also a foreigner in Egypt and I was afraid that my true story would not be believed. Meanwhile, my mind was racing: where was Yasmeen? Where were the boys?

The men had left me in the street. They had taken the money and run. They were capable of anything. They were capable of selling Yasmeen back to the family. I was lost: having lost my children, I was losing my life.

But the strength of my survival instinct surprised me, and I fought hard to hold on. And I watched the policeman carefully as I answered his questions, making sure that he wrote everything down. I didn't want my efforts and information to go for nothing. I felt myself slipping away again, and I reached out to hold the policeman's hand. I was afraid that if I lost consciousness I might never wake up again. 'Hold my hand,' I said to him. 'I'm afraid.'

There was a commotion at the door behind my head and I tried to turn, hoping that it was the doctor arriving. It was the grandfather! And beside him was Effet, the children's stepmother.

He's come back to finish me off.

'Where is Yasmeen?' he demanded. 'Where is Yasmeen?' echoed Effet. She had lost my daughter, her charge – and she was terrified of the consequences for herself. She showed no concern about my injuries. I stared at them in utter disbelief. I pointed to the grandfather and said to the policeman: 'That's him. That's the man who stabbed me.' My handprints – in my blood – were on his jacket.

Then things seemed to be happening in slow motion. I saw his feet near my head, saw him take aim. I turned my face away and his foot crashed into the back of my head as he poured out a venomous stream of abuse: 'You prostitute! You daughter of dirt!'

The policeman got to his feet and pulled a gun from his

holster, pointing it at the grandfather. Then he forced the grandfather and Effet out of the hut while I lay on the floor groaning in pain and indignation.

I was intensely relieved when the policeman came back and crouched down next to me. He held my hand while we waited for the ambulance. I could see the fear in his eyes: he thought that I was going to die in front of him. He began to go through my handbag, and I knew that he was looking for identification. He took out my passport and telephone index and I grabbed them back from him. Medhat's telephone number was in the book and I didn't want him implicated. I put my passport inside the telephone index and held it to my body.

But the policeman was getting increasingly nervous about my deteriorating condition and promising that he would return immediately, he went outside. He returned quickly with two men and ordered them to carry me to a waiting taxi; he was not going to wait any longer. I was lifted on to a bedsheet and carried to the taxi. I cried out in pain as the jerky movements of the men opened my wounds up still further. 'Come with me,' I asked the policeman, but he said he had to stay at the hotel and make a report.

The taxi sped very fast down the rough Cairo streets and every bump made me yelp with agony. The driver apologized to me all the way: 'Ma lesh Ya Madam. You are very ill and we must get to the hospital fast.'

And then finally we were slowing down and coming to a halt. I was lifted on to a trolley and there were medical staff all around me. 'Are you a doctor?' I asked in Arabic of the nearest man to me. He smiled down at me and spoke in English: 'Yes I am. You are safe now, don't worry.'

And then we were rushing, rushing down a corridor, a

doctor by my head, another doctor at the foot of the trolley, running as they pushed me along, shouting out orders: 'Hurry up! Get out of the way!'

A mask was pushed over my head as we rushed, but I forced it off. I needed to pray: 'Stay with me God, stay with me.' Under the bright lights of the operating theatre I begged the doctor to put me to sleep. The pain was unbearable. I could smell blood; I could taste blood.

'In just one moment,' he answered me, very kindly.

Waiting for the anaesthetic, I still wanted to explain what happened: 'I tried to rescue my children. They were kidnapped. Do you know where my children are?'

The doctor didn't answer. The medical team was working swiftly and silently except for the voice of the doctor at my feet who was issuing orders.

'Oh God, it hurts too much, please put me to sleep,' I asked the doctors. And then my arm was being held and the doctor was saying, 'OK, here we go, you can go to sleep now.'

I watched the needle going into my hand and waited for the relief of oblivion. And I heard someone saying: 'Your daughter is safe; she is in the British Embassy.'

And then I drifted off into a world of indifference.

Chapter Four

My eyes stayed closed but I could hear people talking around me and I knew that I was in a hospital. I knew the reason why I was there, but I didn't know how long I had been unconscious.

Where were my children?

I suffered the agony of not being able to surface back to full consciousness while I relived all that had happened. I saw my sons running away from me. I saw the grandfather knifing me and I saw the six-lane road stretching before me. Had I imagined it, or had someone told me that Yasmeen was in the Embassy?

I tried hard – but failed – to open my eyes. I was angry with myself: I had important questions in my mind that needed urgent answers. Part of me was restless and eager to get on, but whenever I came close to the surface, I drifted off again.

Although I was only unconscious for twenty-four hours, it seemed like weeks before I broke through – to find doctors and nurses surrounding my bed and smiling at me. I was wired to a drip and I was in terrible pain. It was 12 December 1990.

It was hard work just to breathe, but I had to have answers to my questions: 'Where are my children?' I wheezed, 'where is my daughter?' A doctor answered me: 'Yasmeen is fine. She is waiting for you in the British Embassy.'

I floated off to sleep again, but found no peace. My mind was tormented by images of my sons. I could see Sammie, naked in a Cairo street, being beaten by his grandfather with a long stick. Sawy's face appeared in front of me, distorted with fear, and he was screaming in terror: 'Mummeeee!! Mummeee!!' When I next came to, my feeling of failure was overwhelming.

I have failed my sons.

Tears flowed down my face and I began to cough violently. Each coughing spasm racked me with fresh pain, and threatened to break the stitches that held my torn body together. Doctors and nurses rushed to my bedside and I tried to talk to them through my tears and pain. A firm voice spoke to me from a distance, telling me to rest, and I was sedated.

It seemed like only seconds later that I was woken by stinging pains that shot through me as sharply as the knife that had almost ended my life. A nurse was cleaning my wounds and I cried like a baby, begging her to stop. I hadn't noticed that there was a doctor present until he spoke to me: 'Don't cry, you are a very strong lady.'

I recognized his face immediately. He was the doctor who had pushed me to the operating theatre. He introduced himself: 'I am Dr Sammie Ramzy, don't you remember me?'

'Yes, I do. You saved my life, didn't you?'

He said to me: 'You are a fighter. A very strong lady. You helped me!'

Dr Sammie examined me, pointing to my body as though it were a map to be explored. He began to explain all that he had done in surgery: 'I didn't have to extend the largest wound; I just put my hand in and stitched up your liver.'

He had also done internal stitches on two broken ribs, but when he told me that he had left two wounds open to drain, I had heard enough. I wasn't ready for the details.

'Don't tell me any more please!' I said. 'It's making me feel worse.' He laughed and changed the subject: 'You are a heroine now! You are our celebrity.' The story of how I had rescued Yasmeen and of the attack on my life had made headlines across Egypt.

I asked him who was caring for Yasmeen while I was in hospital. He told me that my sister Kath – who lives in Croydon – had arrived in Cairo to look after Yasmeen, and that Kath would be coming to see me later that day. It was wonderful news. I couldn't wait to see her, but I knew that the news of my attack would have taken its toll on her and I worried about how she had been affected.

Dr Sammie was looking at me pensively and he said: 'The man that did this to you is not human. He has no heart. He is an animal.' He told me to rest, saying that he would be back to check on me later. I dozed peacefully, waiting for my loving sister to arrive.

And then suddenly, there she was, her face lined with worry, hurrying towards my bed. We wrapped our arms around each other in the warmest embrace, and Kath spoke to me in simple terms of love: 'Oh Pammy! I thought I'd never see you again. I love you so much!' She smelled of home and of comfort; in her arms I found safety. Safety to sob. Safety to unleash my anger and desperate, desperate sadness. Safety to release emotions that I had suppressed from the day that my children had been stolen from me.

I wept and wailed while Kath held me tightly to stop me from falling apart. My emotions were so ferocious that they frightened me. I felt like an angry volcano that had been waiting to erupt for a long, long time. An audience of nurses had gathered outside, and soon they were all in tears too. Kath sat on my bed, holding my hand and crooning soothing words to me. Her loving voice showered me with balm, and I began to feel a little better.

Kath told me of the uncanny way that she had learned about my stabbing. Acting on intuition – she had a strong feeling that something had happened to me – she had called the British Embassy in Cairo on the very morning that I had been attacked. She had spoken to Helen Holmes, who told her that I was in hospital and that Yasmeen was at the Embassy. Distraught, Kath had flown out to Cairo the same day. Her voice was still hoarse from sobbing as she told me: 'Oh Pam, I prayed to God all the way here on the plane.'

I had so much that I wanted to say to her, so many questions to ask, but every time I tried to talk, I dissolved into tears again. But Kath knew me so well that she anticipated my questions and answered them. She told me of Yasmeen's excitement at seeing her Auntie again after fourteen months; of how Yasmeen had squealed with joy and thrown herself into Kath's lap. And she told me of Yasmeen's delight at scoffing down cream-filled Easter eggs after so long. It was typical of Kath to remember Yasmeen's favourite sweets and to take the time to buy them for her, even in the midst of such emotional turmoil and frantic travel arrangements. She was so thoughtful and kind; it was easy to see why she had been nicknamed 'Angel' by our father.

Kath also told me of the public outcry after the news of my attack had hit the headlines in Britain. 'Everyone is so angry,' she said, 'I just hope that something will be done now.' We both felt that something positive must come out of my suffering. Surely it was now quite clear that the children should be with me and not with their violent grandfather? Surely the Egyptian authorities would step in and sort this problem out?

When Dr Sammie came around to see me with a nurse to clean my wounds again, Kath refused to leave my bedside. I tried hard not to cry, not wanting to upset Kath any further, but I couldn't help it. And when Kath saw my injuries she too broke down: 'Oh my God, look what that evil man has done! I hope he goes to hell!'

Dr Sammie put a comforting arm around Kath's shoulder. And for the first time I found the courage to look at my injuries. It was my turn to be horrified and angry. My body was a mass of jagged wounds and stitches as if train tracks had criss-crossed my abdomen. All I could say was, 'How dare he! How dare he!'

There were strange ring marks under my breast and in the centre of my chest that looked like burns. Dr Sammie explained that the marks were from the electric shock therapy that had been necessary when my heart had failed three times during surgery. I was beginning to understand how very lucky I was to be alive – and how much gratitude I owed to Dr Sammie. My sister's eyes were brimming with tears as she searched for the right words with which to thank him.

Then Kath noticed that my feet and toes were caked with dried blood and she asked the nurse for warm water to bathe me. Her tears dropped on to my feet as she gently cleaned me, and she said: 'It's too much! First Daddy dying (after an illness six months previously); then the children being stolen, and now this. I sometimes wonder how we have all got through this far.' I wished I could console her and lift the sorrow that was written all over her face, but I couldn't find the words.

Kath told me that Helen Holmes was looking after Yasmeen in her absence, and that Helen would be in to see me the next day. We sat holding hands, quietly talking for a while, and then it was time for Kath to leave. I was desperately tired, and I slept peacefully for the first time in a long while.

The next day, 13 December, Helen Holmes arrived, and fussed over me like a mother hen, fluffing my pillows and straightening my bed. She insisted on washing my face and brushing my hair. 'Don't bother,' I said, 'it'll take a miracle to make me look better!' But she wouldn't listen.

When she felt she'd fussed enough, she sat and talked to me: 'Your daughter!' she exclaimed. 'She's just like you. Talks incessantly. Can't stop her!' She made me laugh with funny stories about Yasmeen and I begged her, 'Helen, no, don't make me laugh. It hurts!'

On a more serious note, Helen told me that the grandfather had been arrested and she warned me that I was soon to be interviewed by the Public Prosecutor. My lawyer and the British Pro-Consul, Youssef Fouad, would also be present at the interview and if I became too tired at the interview, I should say so.

The next day, impatient to make a fast recovery, I got up to use the bathroom. Two nurses, horrified that I should even try, held me under each arm as I walked to the bathroom. I got there all right, but I couldn't get back. My strength failed me and a wheelchair had to be brought to ferry me back to bed. The nurses clucked and tutted and threatened to tie me to the bed.

I resolved to try again later, foolishly assuming that my convalescence was the same as at other times in hospital when I had given birth to my beautiful babies. When no nurses were about, I crept out into the corridor and managed to shuffle about ten yards before I heard a nurse shout out to me, 'Ya Afreeta!' (You spirit!). She ran to me and caught me just before I fell. This time one of the doctors came to scold me, but after listening to my pleas, he agreed that I could try to walk a little further each day – on the condition that I wouldn't try to walk alone.

That afternoon, the Public Prosecutor interviewed me. It was quite an ordeal; I was worried about implicating Medhat and the men in my team. True, the men had left me in the street to be almost murdered, but they had helped me to recover Yasmeen.

But I was exhausted by my earlier expedition to the bathroom, and I fell asleep in the middle of their intensive questioning. My doctors asked the Public Prosecutor, my lawyer and the British Pro-Consul to leave the room and finish the questioning on another day.

As time passed and I gradually gained strength, more and more telegrams, cards and flowers arrived by my bedside and the switchboard was busy with calls from well-wishers. Journalists also arrived at the hospital to see me, but they were turned away by the Egyptian police who had been posted on the hospital doors to protect me against possible further attacks from my ex-husband's family.

Kath and Helen visited me every day, bringing me letters and loving messages from my little princess Yasmeen. On 14 December she wrote:

Dear Mummy,

I love you and I'm worried about you. You are part of me like I am part of you. I promise I'll never leave you again. I asked you to take me away from my grandparents and you did, a favour which I'll always remember. Anyway, good luck, and I hope you get better quickly. Lots of love and millions of kisses and prayers for getting better soon,

Yasmeen.

Every letter made me more determined to get better fast to be reunited with her quickly.

Kath explained to me that she had to return to Britain, but that our sister Queenie was coming to take over the job of caring for Yasmeen. The day that Kath said goodbye was as emotional as the day that she had arrived. She left this letter for Yasmeen:

My Dear Yasmeen,

I am writing to you at 4.30 in the morning before I go to the airport to fly to London. When I've gone, Auntie Queenie will come to Egypt to be with you.

I know it's very hard for you at the moment because you wanted to leave grandfather but now you are in the Embassy and not with Mummy, but it is only for a little while. I am going to write down all the days until Christmas for you, and you can cross one off every night and then you will know when Christmas day comes.

I love you very much and I hope that you really know that in your heart and feel safe because your family loves you and the Embassy is doing a lot of things to help you and Mummy.

I am going soon, and I will come and kiss you in bed before I go.

Lots of love and hugs from Auntie Kathy. XXXX

Kath also left me this letter to read when she had gone:

My Darling Pammy,

A message for you when I have gone. I love you more than words can say, and I'm so angry about what's happened to you – but we all have to hold on to that for now.

God Almighty spared your life. I prayed for you on the plane, pleading with God to let me see you when I arrived. Thank you God!

Just try to get better, and not to think about too much else.

I love you Pam.

Kath

She was gone, but her love stayed with me and comforted me even in her absence. Kath and I had always been very close, sharing an almost supernatural, telepathic kind of communication, and now we had become even closer.

My sister Queenie was due in Cairo very late that night and was coming to see me the next day. But when she was late arriving at the hospital I had an uneasy feeling that something was not right. A warning bell was ringing loudly in my head. I tried to reason with myself and shake the feeling off, but in the end I followed my instincts. I went to the desk outside the ward and told the doctor on duty that I had to phone the British Embassy.

As I waited for the switchboard to give me a line, I suddenly knew that my ex-husband was at the Embassy. My hands were shaking as I dialled the number. I got through to the Consular Section and spoke to Helen: 'Is everything all right?' I asked her. 'Ye-es . . ,' she answered me in a tone of voice that I had heard before. It was her 'calmly dealing with an emergency' voice.

Helen put Queenie on the line and Queenie's voice was

full of panic. 'He's there, isn't he?' I said to her. 'Yes,' she answered, 'he's come for Yasmeen.' I became frantic: 'Queenie, don't let her go! Don't let him take her!' She tried to calm me down: 'Don't be stupid,' she said, 'of course we're not going to let her go.'

But fear was sweeping over me and I gasped for breath while my heart beat wildly and irregularly. The doctor gently but firmly took the phone from my hand and spoke to my sister, while a nurse led me back to my bed. They scolded me for getting overexcited, but how could I relax when there was a danger of losing my daughter? And what about Yasmeen? She must have been terrified. After all that we had been through, were the Embassy going to be forced to hand over my little princess?

I sat up in bed, rattling with nerves, jumping every time the phone rang. Fortunately I didn't have to wait long before Helen called. I hardly gave her time to answer my questions: 'Helen, what happened? What did he say? Is he still there?'

'Pam, calm down!' Helen told me. 'It's no good for you to get so worked up. It's OK,' she went on. 'He's gone. I told him to buzz off.'

When my ex-husband had come to the Embassy to demand she give his daughter back, Helen had asked him if he had a court order for the return of Yasmeen. He claimed he did have a court order – but that it wasn't with him at that moment. Helen had said to him: 'You go away and bring me your court order, and then we'll talk again. But don't ever come back here without it!'

I was so relieved that I couldn't stop thanking Helen. I asked if Yasmeen was OK, and Helen said that she had been very shaky, but that she was recovering. Helen also told me that Queenie was on her way to the hospital in an

Embassy car. And then she gave me *my* orders: 'Go and lie down, now! And for God's sake keep calm!'

When Queenie bounced into the ward she was all hyped up and dying to tell me what had happened. But first, big hugs! We couldn't let go of each other; it was a lovely feeling. She kissed me and kissed me, and I kept telling her over and over that I loved her. We three sisters are as different as can be, yet we share a deep love and fierce loyalty to each other.

Queenie had so much to tell me. She and Yasmeen had been walking through the Embassy grounds towards the tennis courts when Yasmeen shouted, 'Auntie Queenie, there's my daddy!' At first Queenie thought Yasmeen was imagining things, and had told her not to be silly. But Yasmeen was right and her father was at the gatehouse, calling her to him. Queenie and Yasmeen had turned and run. When they got back to the Consular Section, said Queenie, Yasmeen was shaking from head to foot.

Yasmeen was keen to know when I was coming out of hospital, Queenie told me, and was upset that she could not visit me. On 16 December, she wrote this letter:

Dear Mummy,

I can't wait any longer to see you. Please tell Auntie Helen to take me to visit you at the hospital. I have to visit you, or don't you want me to see you? I can't wait, please Mummy,

Lots of love,

Yasmeen

I wrote back immediately to explain that, as much as I would love her to visit, she was only safe within the British Embassy walls while my ex-husband's family was still trying to get her back. Yasmeen was also fretting about how we were going to get a birthday present to her brother Sawy on Christmas Eve. What could I say to her? I could think of no way of getting a present to him.

It was 17 December, just six days after I had been attacked. Helen came to see me with news that made me very nervous. The Embassy had sought legal advice on Yasmeen's safety within the Embassy — which is technically British sovereign soil. Helen explained that while I was not with Yasmeen, the Embassy could not guarantee her safety. If Abdel-Salam came up with a court order, they might be forced to give her up to her father.

The news made my mind up. I had to go to Yasmeen. I couldn't take any chances with losing her again. I knew that she would be severely punished by her father and grandparents if she was returned to them. And I had to be with Yasmeen at Christmas.

When Helen had gone I spoke to one of the doctors and told him of the latest news about Yasmeen's safety. I begged him to discharge me and he promised to talk to the Chief Consultant of Heliopolis Hospital, Dr Samir Sultan.

Dr Samir came to see me the next morning and he was full of smiles: 'You are a star!' he said, 'and we are moving you to a private room downstairs.' I was taken in a wheelchair down long corridors and into a beautiful room with a balcony, private shower and telephone. There was a magnificent display of flowers by my bed, sent by a well-wisher, and a card that read, 'All of Egypt is with you: please get well soon.'

I sat on the balcony and watched people walking in the streets. I could hear cars and the wonderful sounds of everyday life. I thought: 'My God, I have survived. I came so close to dying and to never seeing or hearing all of this.' I listened to the call to prayer from a nearby mosque and I thanked God for my life.

Then I picked up the phone and called Yasmeen. She was delighted to hear my voice: 'Mummy! Mummy, when are you coming home,' she said. 'I am afraid; maybe Daddy can take me back?' I tried to reassure her, promising that we would spend Christmas together, but I could tell that she was not convinced.

Hearing the desperation in Yasmeen's voice made me even more determined to leave the hospital quickly. I called for Dr Sammie Ramzy and explained that I would not be able to recover fully in hospital where I was racked with fears for my daughter's safety. I promised him that I would return to the hospital every day for an examination and that I would rest at the Embassy, cared for by Queenie and Yasmeen. At last he agreed to think about it, and he promised to tell me his decision in the morning.

That evening Queenie came to see me, and with her was my lawyer of the time (Ibrahim Anous) plus a friend of his who was a High Court Judge. My lawyer believed that Yasmeen was safe in the Embassy, but warned me that I should not take her out of Egypt without the permission of a Judge – in case that jeopardized my chances of winning custody of Sammie and Sawy.

He was adamant that we shouldn't travel without permission, and then he said: 'But don't worry dear lady. We have a judge here with us who will do everything for you.' I understood. Months of dealing with people who offered me 'solutions' in return for money had taught me well. My lawyer and his friend the Judge were looking for a bribe, trading on my despair and the desperate situation of my children.

I simply said: 'I'm too ill to think of that now; I'm just trying to get better.' Before they left my room, my lawyer leaned towards me and said: 'Where did you find those men that you hired? They are stupid men. You should have come to me; I would have found you real men.'

I answered him: 'Because if I had come to you for that kind of help you would have said to me, "No, don't think of using force, the law is with you." But in fact we all know that the law doesn't give a damn about my children.'

After they had gone I told Queenie what had been said. She thought it was marvellous that they had offered to help Yasmeen and me out of Egypt. I tried to explain to her that they only wanted money. In fourteen months I had been learning the hard way who could – and could not – be trusted. This system of bribes and contacts was a world away from all that Queenie knew back home in England.

When Queenie had gone I sat on the balcony, breathing the air that I felt so lucky to breathe. I plugged in the personal stereo that Kath had sent me from London and listened to the tape inside. Kath had recorded Capital Radio and I could hear traffic bulletins about the A40 together with familiar music which reminded me of my identity.

Kath had recorded it with a motive and her message came through loud and clear: 'This is where you belong. Get on with it!' For the first time in a week I started to plan the future, making notes about what I had to do. I was back to the work of getting my children home again.

Chapter Five

On 19 December, I woke up early. There was no time to waste: I planned to look very much better when Dr Sammie arrived to tell me of his decision. I hadn't washed my hair for nine days and it no longer hung on my head; it jutted out in the most unexpected ways.

I climbed out of bed with a feeling of renewed energy. I couldn't wait to get myself dressed up. I opened the curtains to let in the sunshine, went towards the shower – and looked at my reflection in the mirror with disbelief. I looked old. This attack, I realized, had almost certainly shortened my life. Would I ever fully recover?

I made a decision to ignore my mirror image. It wasn't me, it was a negative of me and I am not a negative person. I kneeled on the floor by the bath, and despite the pain caused by leaning over, I began to wash my hair. To my horror, great lumps of hair fell from my head and into the bath. It was a consequence of the trauma of the attack and subsequent surgery. I refused to let it get me down, and wrapping my head in a towel, I put on my make-up and tied my hair back into a low pony-tail. When I had finished I looked in the mirror; I was the image of a defiant clown.

Dr Ashraf Hammouda came into my room and was clearly shocked (*anyone* would have been shocked), but he said to me 'Ay da! Ay El-Gameel da! What is this? What is this beauty?'

Then Dr Samir Sultan came into the room puffing on a cigarette and I said to him, 'You are supposed to be a doctor, how can you smoke in front of a patient?' He looked at me with a mock stern expression and said, 'OK, you can go to your daughter!'

I threw my arms around his neck and kissed him, celebrating my release, my survival and my success in recovering my daughter all at the same time. As we hugged he whispered in my ear, 'Ya Afreeta!'

Dr Ashraf was still with me when Dr Sammie Ramzy came to say goodbye. What could I say to these two men who had saved my life? I could not thank them enough, but I made them promise to visit Yasmeen and me at the British Embassy.

When I telephoned the Embassy with my good news Helen said to me 'If you die, I'll kill you!' but I knew that she was pleased. Then I spoke to Yasmeen who was very excited: 'I can't wait for you to come home, Mummy,' she said, 'the flat at the Embassy is fantastic, it's like being in England.'

Queenie had told me how much Yasmeen was enjoying her new-found freedom. She had befriended Yvette, an Egyptian girl working at the Embassy. Yasmeen had installed herself in Yvette's office and was 'working' furiously at the typewriter all day, learning keyboard skills and making telephone calls. I was heartened to hear that my daughter had not lost her irrepressible spirit and I could hardly wait to be reunited with her. But at the same time, I was afraid.

I could only imagine all that Yasmeen had been through in the past fourteen months. I knew that she had been beaten. I knew that her grandparents had tried to have her circumcised. I knew that her father had told her that if I came to Cairo he would have me killed and buried in a secret place.

My children had been stolen from me at a crucial time in their development. At such young ages, children are like tiny sponges, open to misinformation and brainwashing. I had no doubt that Yasmeen had been told a lot of lies about me.

When my ex-husband took the children to Cairo, he had told them that I had gone mad and been locked in an insane asylum for ever. He and the grandparents had repeatedly told the children that I was a prostitute, that I didn't love them and that I only wanted them back so that I could keep my council house in Mitcham. What other appalling stories had been planted in their minds?

When adult prisoners like the Beirut hostages are released after long months or years of captivity, specialist doctors and therapists are made available by governments to assess their mental distress and to help them to readjust to normal life. But abducted children and their families get no such support.

I had rescued Yasmeen on my own initiative, and I knew that I alone would have to deal with the long-term effects and repercussions of her abduction. No child should have to cope with the kind of experiences she had been through. Not long after I rescued her, she wrote this account of what happened that day with a child's clarity – but also with a painful knowingness beyond her nine years:

On December 11th 1990, I remember coming out of the house. I remember how I felt when sort of skipping down the steps out of my front door. I felt quite funny really, excited, and then I looked behind me to see who was there. It was Sawy. Sammie was holding my grandfather's hand because my grandfather's hand was warm.

I also remember waving a second goodbye to Effet Shadid, my Daddy's second wife, and my grandmother (Atoof Torkey). Then, quite cold, I walked off beside my brothers. I knew my mother was coming to get me but I didn't know when. I walked faster and faster because of the cold.

I remember seeing a man in a red jacket buying fowl and taamaya (a bean and herb burger) from a man at a stall and another buying eggs and pickles and eating them. I looked to the other side of me where there was a closed, red sort of supermarket where they sold chickens, ice cream and eggs, drinks, tins of things and frozen vegetables and frozen pitta bread.

I knew the man who worked there; he was nice and I know him because me and Effet went there for our food. I wanted to see if it was open so I could say hello to him or his wife.

As soon as I stopped looking I started talking to my grandfather saying, 'Throw a stone at one of the dogs if they're there, because you know that I'm afraid of them.' Then Sawy called me a scaredy cat so I just said that he was one too.

Then I stopped. A car went past. I started walking again, then suddenly a car just like a black-and-white taxi swooped around me, well, in front of me. Then I heard a skidding noise. I saw a woman that I hadn't seen before in that place by the front left side of the black taxi.

She shouted out loud and clear; 'Yasmeen, get in the car, we're going on holiday.' I kind of froze with shock. Then someone from behind me pushed me and got me into the car, closed the door and jumped into the front seat and said, 'Ma lesh ya Mohammed', and said to me in Arabic, 'Are you OK?'

I said 'Yes, but I think I've left my shoe behind.' He said, 'Don't worry, we will buy you a new pair,' so I hoped that I had lost it.

I suddenly looked behind me and all I saw was my brother Sawy standing quite straight, leaning on one foot with his head slightly tilted to the side, with his mouth half open half closed. And Sammie, with both knees bent one in front of the other, both arms beside him, mouth closed as if about to run.

Then it struck me and I said in Arabic, 'Where is my mother?' He said, 'She is coming.' Then I said out of worry and to impress the driver, 'Oh my God, what about Effet? She will be worried!'

So the driver said, 'Well, do you want to go back to your grand-father because we don't want to do anything you don't want to do.' So I said, 'No, take me to Helen, my Mum's friend in the British Embassy.'

They stopped off on the way and bought me loads of chocolates and sweets and then stopped off again and bought some mint tea.

We finally got to the Embassy. I saw Mrs Helen Holmes there and another girl called Azza. I was well cared for in the Embassy. Auntie Helen gave us a flat; it was like a massive villa all fitted into one room. It didn't have a telly, but it was very very nice and I appreciated it very much.

In the morning, the British Embassy sent a chauffeur and a bodyguard, and I felt very pampered. The chauffeur wel-comed me warmly: 'Ahlan! Ahlan ya Madam!' On the way to the Embassy we went through Abbassia and I told Queenie that this is where I had been living in recent months. She turned her nose up and said: 'I don't know how you've managed all this time, Pam. I couldn't live there.'

And as we drove through the Cairo streets it was as if I were watching the events of the past fourteen months again, but with a different perspective, as if it were a film. Queenie noticed that my mind was far away and said, 'Don't think about it now, Pam.'

The Embassy gates were a familiar and reassuring sight. On that day the Embassy meant safety, sanctuary and a long-awaited reunion with my daughter. As we drove inside the gates, the Egyptian staff were waiting to greet me. I knew them all well and I was touched by their warmth and concern as one by one they came to shake my hand and say, 'Welcome back, Madam'.

And then I was being helped out of the car and Queenie was holding my arm, walking me to the stairs that lead to the Consular Section. But the same stairs that I had run down only ten days ago now presented an almost insurmountable challenge. It took me fifteen minutes to climb the staircase. Dr Sammie had told me that it would take at least a year for me to recover. I hadn't believed him at the time, but now I changed my mind.

I was wheezing and breathless when I got to the top. Helen was waiting for me. 'Yasmeen?' I managed to gasp. 'She's upstairs in the flat,' Helen said, 'and it's just as well. You can't let her see you like that, Pam, she's been through enough already.'

I was painfully aware of how awful I looked. My teeth felt loose and wobbly and there seemed to be huge gaps between them. My hair was straw-like and I was walking stooped over from the pain of my wounds. I looked like a frail and ageing woman, closer to fifty-five than thirty-five.

As I sat recovering my breath, I heard Helen suggest to Queenie that I put some make-up on to avoid frightening Yasmeen. Helen brought me a glass of water and I joked with her: 'Make-up isn't enough Helen; what I need is a face transplant.'

I had more stairs to climb to get to the flat on the second floor, and I took them very slowly, not wanting to be breathless when I faced Yasmeen. But the door to the flat opened before Queenie had a chance to use her key. It was Yasmeen: what a feast for my hungry eyes! She looked so tiny; so sweet; so very edible!

'Yasmeeny!' was all that I could blurt out. 'Mummy!' she said, 'Mummy, welcome home!' But her face showed distress and I knew that my appearance had scared her. She later told a journalist of her feelings:

I was really shocked when I saw her. She could hardly speak, her teeth were black and her hair was all dry. She was also really weak. I thought she had been stabbed with a penknife and I didn't know how bad it was. But the first time I saw her scars I had to run away and couldn't talk for a while.

I was afraid to cuddle her; afraid to get too close to her for fear of scaring her more. 'I'm all right Yasmeen,' I said to her softly, 'I'm much better now, and I'll soon look like me again.' I suddenly felt completely drained and I knew that I had to sit down before I fell over.

'Show me the living room then,' I said to Yasmeen. Glad of the chance to do something she took my hand and guided me to the spacious, elegant living room. She was so proud of her new home and she wanted to show me everything all at once. 'Look Mum,' she said, 'I know how to draw the curtains!' She pulled the cord to draw the curtains across the tall French windows and, just as quickly, she snapped them open again.

She was enjoying herself, but she wouldn't look directly at me and I knew that she was disappointed in the way I looked. Queenie took control: 'Let's make Mummy a cup of tea shall we?' Then she took Yasmeen into the kitchen while I sat looking at my elegant surroundings.

Yasmeen called to me: 'Mum, come and see the kitchen.' I heard my sister say that Mummy was tired, but I couldn't disappoint my girl. I got up and walked towards them. The kitchen was well equipped with a fridge, freezer and electric cooker, luxuries that Yasmeen and I had not seen for a long time.

Yasmeen opened and shut everything, delighted to reveal the contents of the freezer to me: 'Fish fingers! Beefburgers! Are you hungry Mummy?' She wouldn't stop talking and couldn't keep still. I was worried: when was she going to calm down? I knew that she was reacting to all the terrible shocks she had suffered and I felt powerless to help her.

I tried to stop the tears that were filling my eyes, but I couldn't. Queenie came and put a loving arm around my shoulders, and Yasmeen rushed to me, arms outstretched. She didn't say a word; she just held me. It was an extraordinary experience for us both: daughter was comforting mother. The months that we had been parted disappeared as we clung to each other.

I said to Yasmeen: 'I can say anything I want to you now, and you can say anything that you want to me. There is no one to tell us "Don't!"' We sat at the kitchen table to drink our tea, and at last, we began to relax a little.

When Helen came up to the flat to visit us, we all sat beaming at each other and joking. But after a while, Helen asked to speak to me alone. We went into the living room and she handed me an official typed letter from the Embassy. I knew it couldn't be good news from the concerned look on Helen's face. The letter told me I would have to leave the flat within two weeks. British diplomatic staff were shortly arriving in Cairo and the flat had been designated to them. I was completely taken aback. My new sense of security had been a false one: I must make plans to fly back to London as soon as possible.

Yet I wasn't going to let anything spoil my first day back with my lovely girl, and so I put the problem firmly to the back of my mind. I would work out my strategy later that night when Yasmeen was firmly tucked up in bed. In England, before the children had been abducted, bedtime had been a battle of wills, but I was amazed at how easy it was that night. When I told Yasmeen it was bedtime, she immediately said, 'Harda' (certainly). I wondered what kind of treatment she had received to make her so sub-missive.

I checked on her later to make sure that she was asleep. It felt so good to act as a mother again. And then I asked Queenie to come with me to the bathroom so that I could clean my wounds with the solution that Dr Sammie had given me. I knew I couldn't perform the task alone: it was too horrible.

We tiptoed to the bathroom and closed the door. The door wouldn't lock, but I wasn't worried; Yasmeen was fast asleep in the bedroom. I lifted my loose clothes gingerly, afraid to look at the damage to my body now that I was away from the safety of the hospital. It was the first time that Queenie had seen my gashes, and she stared open-mouthed.

I felt awfully sorry for myself and I tried to take control, but it was useless. I heard myself whimpering like a child, and suddenly realized that I cried in exactly the same way as my little sunny Sammie-boy. In my mind, my whimpering became his and there was nothing which could comfort me. Queenie was sniffing and crying and saying to me, 'Poor Pammy, you look just like you did when you were little.' She held me in her arms while I sobbed, 'Queenie, I cry like Sam! I can hear him!'

She begged me not to torture myself and to concentrate on getting well, but all I could hear was Sammie's voice crying out for his Mum and pining for the comfort that only my arms could give him. I didn't even try to stop my tears; I wanted to cry; I needed to cry.

My body had been vandalized by a vicious, violent man and I cried in anger, I cried against injustice, I cried remembering the children lost to me. I felt such indignation and jealousy that the two children born of my body were still with the man who had stuck the knife in my belly.

So engrossed was I in my own grief – and Queenie in her own shock – that we didn't notice Yasmeen standing behind us in the bathroom. I turned around to comfort her, forgetting that my wounds were exposed. She was leaning against the tiled wall of the bathroom, her hands clasped behind her back. Her face was statue-like and her eyes were vacant. I watched my little girl slide down the wall in a faint. I tried to lift her, but I could not. I tried to talk to her, but my words went into nowhere. I witnessed my child of spirit losing her spirit – and that was the moment that the urge to fight returned to me. I would find the strength to set my emotions aside for a while longer in order to get Yasmeen back on an even keel. I could not do that in Egypt while we lived in continuing insecurity and danger. I had to get Yasmeen home to the country of her birth.

Queenie lifted Yasmeen and carried her to the bedroom, while I hurriedly put on a nightgown. I went as fast as I could to the bedroom to find Yasmeen awake and talking to Queenie: 'Hate! Hate! I hate him!' – and I knew she was talking about her grandfather.

I sat on the bed next to my daughter and I said to her: 'Leave it to me; I'll put him in prison, you'll see. But one thing at a time. I've got to get you safely home first. You just enjoy being back with Mummy, and don't worry about anything.' I would have to stay close to Yasmeen that night, putting off making the travel plans until the next day.

Queenie brought us a bedtime drink and left us alone together. We couldn't cuddle up too close because of my wounds, but Yasmeen put her arm around my neck and sucked her thumb. I used to scold her for thumb-sucking, but that night I was happy to see her doing it. She was still a child, and she was my child.

As she slept I felt her breath on my face. She smelled so sweet; I had forgotten the sweet smell of my children's breath and I savoured every moment of lying there with her. When I was absolutely sure that she was sleeping deeply, I carefully drew myself away from her and got out of bed.

I crept into the living room and made notes about all the things that I had to do to get us out of Egypt. My worst fear was of losing Yasmeen as we tried to leave the country. I had a deep dread of being tapped on the shoulder by an immigration official as we tried to board a plane at Cairo airport and being told, 'This child is not allowed to leave Egypt.'

I was doing nothing illegal in taking Yasmeen home, but I knew that – in Egypt – the law would not be enough to protect us. I had to get my contacts to check the airport computer. I would have to speak to Medhat and arrange for bribes to go to the right officials.

I fell asleep with the pen in my hand, and I woke to see Yasmeen's face beaming down at me. She had my breakfast on a tray, complete with a rose in a bud vase. I felt as though I was being awarded a medal. It was a wonderful start to the day and I climbed out of bed feeling that I could achieve something if I put my mind to it. But I didn't want Yasmeen to overhear my telephone conversations in case she realized that I still had fears for her safety. Queenie understood perfectly and half an hour later I found myself alone in the flat; Auntie and niece had gone for a walk in the grounds.

I went straight to the phone to begin work. Before I picked it up, it rang. It was Helen calling me from her office downstairs: she had seen Queenie and Yasmeen go out and she would let me know when they were on their way back.

She also gave me a list of people who had phoned asking to speak to me. Most of them were journalists from England. Helen had promised to pass on their messages but had refused to give them other information. Helen asked me for the names of those people I was prepared to talk to: the Embassy operator would not connect anyone else to my apartment.

After the official business, Helen spoke to me as a friend: 'Are you all right? We need to sit and talk, Pam.' I told her that I was going to phone Medhat to ask him to use his contacts at the airport. But it was Medhat that she wanted to talk to me about, so I told her I would be down to see her within the hour.

Meanwhile, I phoned Medhat in Abbassia. I wanted to know what had happened on the day that I was stabbed. Where had Medhat been? He didn't ask me how I was feeling: he was clearly sick with worry about being implicated in the snatch. He said that after Yasmeen had got into the car, the men had driven to Abbassia and he had joined them there.

'I didn't know you were stabbed, honestly!' he said. 'I thought you were with the men.' He told me that he had arranged with the men the night before to meet them in the café if anything went wrong. 'So you knew that something had gone wrong then?' I said. 'When did you find out that I had been stabbed?'

Medhat claimed that he did not know until later that morning when he had called the Embassy asking for me. Helen had told him I was dying in hospital (after I had called her from the El-Salam Hotel she had scoured the hospitals of Cairo). Medhat claimed that he fell on the floor in a faint at the news.

He also complained that Ahmed was blackmailing him

for more money, threatening to tell the police that Medhat had helped to snatch Yasmeen. I said, 'Tell Ahmed from me that if he gives you any more trouble, I'll give his name to the Public Prosecutor. That will shut him up.' Then we arranged to meet the next day at the Meridien Hotel to discuss getting Yasmeen through Cairo airport.

After speaking to Medhat, I phoned the airlines to find out about flights from Alexandria airport and other exits from the country. And I rang my senior lawyer: Madiha Luxour, whom Medhat had been working with, who reassured me that taking Yasmeen out of Egypt would have no effect on the outcome·of my custody case. In fact Madiha urged me to get Yasmeen out as soon as possible. (Her advice had become invaluable to me. She was prepared to be frank even when I might not have wanted to hear what she advised and I had come to trust her and rely on her strength and support.)

Then I went downstairs to confer with Helen. She closed her door so that we could talk privately and told me what had happened on the day that I was stabbed. Apparently, Medhat had phoned the Embassy in such a panic that Helen couldn't understand a word he was saying. She passed him on to the Egyptian Pro-Consul to see if he could make any sense of him.

Medhat had said that he had Yasmeen with him, but that he couldn't find me. He asked the Embassy to take Yasmeen in, and within minutes she had arrived at the Embassy with Medhat and the men. Then Medhat had asked Helen for $1,000. He said Ahmed claimed I had not paid him, and that Ahmed had threatened Medhat with violence if he didn't pay up.

Helen first made sure that Yasmeen was safe inside the Embassy grounds. Then she ordered the lot of them out, telling Medhat that if he didn't move fast, he'd have her to contend with! Not surprisingly, they left rather quickly.

Had she told him that I'd been stabbed? 'He already knew you'd been stabbed Pam,' Helen told me. Yasmeen had given Helen this account of what happened: when she had got into the car, Ahmed had asked if she wanted to go back with her grandfather, or would she rather be with her mother? Yasmeen told them to take her to 'Mummy's friend at the Embassy'. Then she had been driven to a place where the men stopped to drink tea.

That was when Medhat had joined them. Yasmeen had asked about me, and Medhat had told her, 'Your grandfather is hitting her.' I found it hard to accept that Medhat had run off, leaving me to be stabbed. But it certainly looked that way.

Queenie and Yasmeen arrived back from their walk in the grounds. Yasmeen was invigorated by her jaunt, but Queenie looked tired out. Yasmeen showed off her new-found independence by picking up the phone in the flat and ordering lunch to be sent over from the Embassy social club.

She had made a lot of friends in the Embassy while I was in hospital. She spoke to the waiter in the Embassy's Oasis Club: 'Hello, is that Mahmoud? It's Yasmeen. Can we have three lunches please, we're all hungry!' Hamburgers and chips arrived very shortly afterwards, delivered by a waiter who was beaming from ear to ear. Yasmeen thanked him in Arabic, promising to bring the plates back to the Club herself. She was loving every minute of her freedom.

After lunch, Queenie told me she had to get back to

London to spend Christmas there with her own daughters. I was disappointed, but I understood. She called the airline and confirmed her seat for the next morning.

I was worried about who would care for Yasmeen when I met Medhat the next day, but Yasmeen put my mind at rest. She told me that she would sit with Yvette in her office in the Consular Section; or, she could go and talk to her new friends in the Oasis Club; or she could watch a video in the TV room . . . She seemed to have it all worked out, so I stopped worrying.

Queenie had to be up early the next morning to catch her flight, but Yasmeen and I were not tired enough for bed. I decided to phone Mohammed Taha, an ex-boyfriend of mine who was living in Cairo and who was one of my ex-husband's friends. I hoped that he would agree to act as a mediator; I felt that Abdel-Salam might be open to negotiation now.

Mohammed told me how sorry he was about all that had happened, and he promised to try to talk to Abdel-Salam. Yet he didn't hold out much hope: he said that Abdel-Salam was very angry with me. '*He's* angry!' I said to Mohammed. 'What about me? I nearly died.' Mohammed promised to call me back when he had news. I let Yasmeen talk to him for a couple of minutes, and she asked him to go and see her brothers on Christmas Eve, explaining that it was Sawy's birthday that day. She asked him to take a message to her brothers, saying how much she loved them.

The next day Queenie was gone, and Yasmeen and I were left alone in the flat. Yasmeen brushed my hair and put it in a pony-tail before I went out: 'Mummy, you look like a little girl!' she said. I took her over to the Oasis Club and settled her in to watch her favourite video, *The Little Mermaid*, and then I was off to meet Medhat.

He was waiting for me, looking around him suspiciously, for all the world like an Egyptian version of Inspector Clouseau. He shook my hand and asked, 'Did anybody follow you?' It was cloak and dagger time again obviously. 'Medhat,' I said, 'calm down, you are drawing attention to yourself. I was driven here in an official Embassy car and nobody followed me.'

While he had a beer and I had a coffee, I explained that Yasmeen and I had to fly home soon and I told him of my fear that Yasmeen could be stopped. Eventually he agreed to talk to his friends at the airport and get the computer checked again. He also told me of what had been happening since the day I was stabbed. Medhat claimed he had been receiving threatening phone calls. A man kept calling up in the middle of the night and threatening to throw acid in his face. He was sure that it was Abdel-Salam. As Medhat drank more beer the story became more dramatic, until it began to sound like the script for a thriller.

I headed back to the Embassy, stopping off to buy sweets for my little princess along the way. She was so involved in the film that she was watching that she didn't notice me at first. I stood back admiring this beautiful creature that was my child, and then she saw me from the corner of her eye: 'Mum!' My favourite name! I was thrilled by her joyful response.

Then her eyes clouded over: 'It's Sawy's birthday tomorrow Mum,' she said quietly. I promised her that we would at least try to speak to him on the phone in the morning.

We went upstairs to our flat and spent the next few hours talking about what had happened to each of us while we had been apart. It was very hard for me to hear from my daughter all that she had suffered, but I had to be careful not to react with too much emotion in case I made her clam up. She told me of how her grandfather beat her regularly with the buckle end of his belt, adding that he always waited until she was undressed. She told me that he used to 'spy' on her, looking around the bedroom door when she changed her clothes after school. She said: 'I don't know why, Mummy, but he used to make me keep the toilet door open and stare at me when I was having a wee.'

In the past months I had managed to make about six visits to the children at their flat, always under the repressive eye of the grandparents. I had always taken presents for the children, but, said Yasmeen, each time the presents had been thrown out as soon as I had gone.

Yasmeen then showed me with her hands how the grandfather had taken out his penis in front of her and her brothers and had rubbed it up and down with both hands. I hid my own hands from her view because they were shaking so much and asked her why she thought he had done that. She said: 'I think it was something to do with teaching the boys to go for a wee-wee.'

One day the grandfather had seen Yasmeen holding hands with a little boy at school: the boy was upset and Yasmeen (who is a little mother hen) had been comforting him. When she got home, the grandfather told her she was 'a prostitute like her mother' – and beat her.

Yasmeen had made friends with a little girl called Meriana. But because she was a Christian, the grandparents wouldn't let her come to the flat. Yasmeen used to play with her in the street instead. But then the grandparents told her that Christians drank blood when they were baptized. Yasmeen was so frightened that she didn't play with her friend any more.

Yasmeen's stepmother Effet had described the act of sexual intercourse in great detail and had told her that if Yasmeen ever had sex, she would die. This, presumably, was to create an aversion to sex in my ten-year-old daughter. I tried to make light of the subject, telling Yasmeen that if that were true, most women would have been dead long ago.

She told me other stories too, of how her brothers were treated. Once, when they had visited their grandmother's sister in Alexandria, the old woman had wanted to kiss Sawy. When he refused, she took a mouthful of water from a glass and spat it in his face.

I asked Yasmeen what did Sawy do? She told me: 'He got up, walked out of the room and went to bed, covering his face because he was crying. He sucked his thumb, and then Granny hit him in the face because she doesn't like him to suck his thumb.'

Yasmeen told me of bad treatment in the children's school also. Sawy had been afraid on the day that all of the children were to be vaccinated and he had sobbed out his fear to Yasmeen. She had gone to the headmistress, begging her not to let her brother be vaccinated without his big sister there to hold his hand. The headmistress had promised to call Yasmeen when it was Sawy's turn, but she had not kept her promise. At playtime, Yasmeen found Sawy in a corner, sucking his thumb and crying for me. He told her that his hands had been tied to the chair with belts while they stuck the needle in him. Yasmeen was crying as she told me all of this, but she insisted on going on. It was as though she was purging herself, emptying out all the things which she had been forced to suppress for so long.

She told me about Sammie, and how he laughed when his grandfather or grandmother hit him: 'Even though it really hurt him, Mummy, he would never cry in front of them. So they hit him harder and harder.' Yasmeen was gasping for breath, but still she went on: 'And then one day he said to Sittee (Granny), "I hate you, I hate you, you fat cow." And then Sittee put paraffin on his head because he had lice and she told him that if he was rude to her again she would set fire to his head.'

It was too much for me. I gulped and retched, fighting hard for control. Yasmeen was saying to me: 'Sorry! Sorry Mummy!' We hung on to each other as Yasmeen tried to console me. She kept saying, 'You'll get them back, don't worry.' We were both so damaged, so tainted by that evil family. But at least we were safe: the boys were not.

Helen came up to the flat and saw that Yasmeen and I looked terrible: our eyes were swollen and our voices were croaky from crying. I told Helen of what Yasmeen had been saying and Helen hugged me close. 'It won't do you any good to think about all that now,' she said. 'You're going to get them back, remember?' Helen had brought us a small Christmas tree and a box full of decorations. There was even a Christmas pudding and a Yule log to cheer us up.

Helen also told me that Dr Nabil Helmy, a criminal lawyer with an excellent reputation, had offered his services to me free of charge. He was a friend of Nawaal Mustapha, the El-Akhbar journalist, and after reading her articles about us he had been so moved that he wanted to help. Helmy offered to represent me in court when the children's grandfather came to trial for attempted murder. Helen gave me his telephone number, and I later met him so that he could take on my case.

Yasmeen and I found ourselves alone again, and I decided to put a brave face on it: 'Let's go out to the Oasis

Club tonight,' I said. 'We'll get all dressed up and have a jolly evening.' Yasmeen brushed my hair and I brushed hers. As a special treat I allowed her to wear nail varnish and a pale pink lipstick, and then I took her down to the Club to relax for a while.

She introduced me to her new friends who worked in the Club. They fussed over her like mad; she was the star of the show and she loved it as much as I loved watching it. But she noticed that I was feeling very tired and said, 'Go and lie down Mummy. I'm safe here, I'll come up in a little while.'

So I went up to the flat and lay on the sofa, resting. When Yasmeen returned she told me that she wanted to speak to her brothers. Tomorrow was Sawy's birthday: 'Maybe Sawy or Sammie will answer the phone,' she pleaded. I couldn't refuse her.

With great presence of mind, Yasmeen had written the telephone number of the grandparents' flat on a scrap of paper and put it in her school bag (together with her poster of Whitney Houston), knowing that I was planning to rescue her. We dialled the number, but there was no reply. We tried the number of the other flat in Sharabiya (I had got hold of that one by ringing friends of the family on the pretext of trying to contact Abdel-Salam). There was no answer there either.

Yasmeen was so disappointed that I didn't know what I could do to console her. Fortunately, our neighbours (British Embassy clerical staff) appeared at the door inviting us in for a drink. They were a lovely couple and Yasmeen and I sat with them watching a video of *Fawlty Towers*. I laughed so much that I had to squash a cushion against my wounds. We went home happy that evening, comforted by a few hours in a family atmosphere, and we climbed into bed and slept almost immediately.

I was woken by the ringing of the telephone. It was Medhat and his voice was tense: 'There is danger and serious problems!' he warned. My blood pressure soared and my heartbeat became erratic. He told me again that he was being threatened and blackmailed. He had paid money to someone to prevent an acid attack upon him – and he was blaming me for his troubles. He went on and on until I was gasping for breath. When he paused to take a breath, he heard my distress – and then handed the telephone to his mother. I heard her shout at her son: 'Haram! (Forbidden by God!) Haram alayk ya Medhat!' She counselled me as I wept, and she simultaneously berated her son.

Then Yasmeen came stomping towards me, her little fists clenched in anger: 'Put the phone down, Mother!' she ordered me. 'Put it down! He is a bastard. He saw you being stabbed, Mother!' She screamed so that he could hear her: 'I hate him! He knew you were being stabbed and I hate him!'

I put my hand over the phone and firmly told her to go back to the bedroom. Then I put the phone to my ear. It was Medhat who spoke this time: 'Your daughter is a bitch! She has no respect for me and she is low class, like her father.' I told him in the clearest terms that I wanted no more to do with him and crashed the phone down defiantly.

Yasmeen had heard my words and she was gleefully clapping her hands and jumping up and down. 'Yes!' she said. 'You told him so Mummy!' I felt victorious but tired and Yasmeen guided me back to bed and offered to make me tea. 'You can't make tea,' I told her, 'you're too little.'

'I know how,' she retorted. 'I had to make tea for Gidou (grandfather) in the mornings and their cooker is really dangerous!' I wouldn't let her make tea, but I let her help me and we sat in the living room sipping our drinks and trying to unwind.

After a while I heard the phone ring again, and I jerked myself up to answer it. I doubled up in pain. I had contracted the tummy muscles that had been torn apart and the shocking pain was a reminder of my frail state. I inched towards the phone, but Yasmeen was there before me. 'It's only Medhat,' she mouthed to me. 'Shall I put the phone down?'

But I shook my head. I knew Medhat would be ringing to apologize. 'I am very sorry,' he said. 'I was very rude to you.' He was calling from the airport where his friend had checked the computer: there was no information there to stop Yasmeen or me from leaving Egypt.

Medhat had also spoken to another friend in immigration. If I went to the airport the next day with £500-worth of gold as a bribe, my passport would be stamped and I would be escorted straight to the plane with Yasmeen. Things were looking up.

I rejoined Yasmeen in the living room – and then I felt a shock go through me. 'What time is it?' I asked Yasmeen. There was a clock in the kitchen: 12.15 a.m. It was 24 December. Christmas Eve. Sawy's birthday.

I held Yasmeen tight in my arms, her head close to my heart, and she asked me in a small, tremulous voice: 'Is it my brother's birthday yet?'

We stood in the kitchen holding each other very tight and we thought only of Sawy Ahmed. Our thoughts, our hearts, our love and our strongest prayers were for him on his birthday. I wondered if he would get a cake with candles. Would he remember the parties that his Mama once did for him?

Did he know where his sister had gone? Did he know if his mother was alive or dead? I drew my sadness inwards and out of view. I sealed my painful sadness away deep inside me, to deal with on another day.

And I rejoiced in the memory of my son's birth. I remembered his beautiful newborn face, his tiny clenched fists and his little lion's roar. I remembered his soft, sensitive soul, and I knew that I would never stop fighting for Sawy or for Sammie.

Chapter Six

On the night of 12 January 1991 Yasmeen and I left the safety of the British Embassy to make ready for our escape from Egypt. I sat in the back of Helen Holmes' car, Yasmeen lying with her head on my lap and covered by a tartan blanket.

Yasmeen's fair hair had been dyed black and bobbed; mine was cut very short. For weeks our photographs had been splashed all over the Egyptian newspapers and I had to avoid our being recognized. I didn't know what Abdel-Salam had been up to with his lawyer. Had he got a court order to stop me taking Yasmeen home? Were his family planning to attack us? I knew that I was not breaking the law in taking Yasmeen home, but in Egypt, with the right bribe, anything can happen.

We stopped, said goodbye to Helen, and took a taxi to the safest haven I knew of: Sittee's home. Yasmeen was very tired and frightened, peering into the dark wet streets for any sign of her father coming to take her away again. I took her slowly up the worn spiral staircase to Sittee's flat, lighting the way with a cigarette lighter.

Sittee was sitting on her makeshift sofa watching the television that was her pride and joy. She opened her arms to Yasmeen and welcomed her warmly: 'Ahlan! Ahlan! Ya, ahlan was Sahlan!' (Welcome, welcome and feel at home.) Sittee hugged and kissed my daughter as if she were her own, but Yasmeen stood stiffly in Sittee's arms, looking around her nervously at the stark, primitive living room.

Sittee tried to comfort Yasmeen, rubbing her back and chanting Koranic verses over her. 'Met-Khafeeshi!' (Don't be afraid) she said to Yasmeen, 'Your mother loves you more than you can imagine and you are safe now!' But it wasn't long before the paraffin heater made Yasmeen drowsy, and she fell asleep sucking her thumb and with her head on Sittee's lap.

Yasmeen woke up in the middle of the night, delirious with fear and calling for me. 'Mummy!' she sobbed, 'I thought I was in Sharabiya!' I sat with her for the rest of the night while she dozed, and at five a.m. I dressed us both. When we heard Medhat's whistle from the street we knew that our taxi had arrived, and we said a sad goodbye to Sittee and made our way down the staircase again.

'We're going home now,' I told Yasmeen, as we arrived at the airport. 'If anyone speaks to you in Arabic, pretend you don't understand.' Medhat had got special permission to enter the airport building; in contrast to British airports, only travellers are normally permitted in Egyptian airport buildings. We had paid for this privilege – together with a safe passage past passport control – with the £500-worth of gold which we had earlier delivered to one of our contacts.

Inside the departure hall, my passport was taken by a man I had never seen before, and within minutes it was returned to me with the necessary stamp. Then an airport official, holding my passport aloft and guiding me by the arm, walked us past the queues of passengers, and with amazing ease we were on the other side of passport control.

We went up the escalators, past the duty free area and waited to board the British Airways Speedbird. I said good-bye to Medhat, thanking him profusely for his help in fixing our passage through the airport – and then we were on our own. I felt that all eyes were on us, and at any moment I expected a policeman to tap me on the shoulder and say, 'You can't take this child out of Egypt!'

I knew that we were not safe until we were on board, airborne and out of Egypt's airspace. Even on the tarmac, it was possible for immigration police to board the plane and take Yasmeen away. The Embassy had also informed me that the aircraft could be turned around when airborne – if Egyptian immigration demanded that Yasmeen be returned to Egyptian soil.

We queued up to board the plane: I held our boarding cards in one of my hands, Yasmeen's hand in the other. There were still twenty people ahead of us in the queue when an Egyptian man in uniform came up to me and said, 'Mrs Ahmed?' I turned to him and hissed a furious 'Yes!' – ready to hit him.

'Could I have your tickets, please,' he said. 'BA's Special Services Desk wish to upgrade your tickets to Club Class!' (They knew I had recently been hospitalized.) Such was my fear that I hadn't noticed that he was wearing a British Airways uniform.

There was only one more immigration check before we boarded. The officer took my passport and began searching through it page by page. 'Where is baby?' he said to me. I grabbed the passport back from him, found the right page and said fiercely to cover up my fear, 'My daughter *Yasmin* is here!' I used the English pronunciation so that he would not think to speak to her in Arabic.

'One minute!' he said, disappearing with my passport. My knees were like jelly – surely we weren't going to be stopped now! – and I held Yasmeen's hand very tightly, trying to fight back the waves of panic. The officer came back, explained to me that there had been no arrivals stamp for Yasmeen – and showed me that his superior had corrected this. I breathed again and put my passport in my bag.

I wanted to run the last few yards to the plane, but I lifted Yasmeen up to show her where the captain sat: 'Look Yasmeen! There's the pilot who is taking us home!' And then we were welcomed on board and seated in the spacious Club Class. Yasmeen looked so tiny in her big chair, and I kept asking her 'Are you all right?' – although it was I who needed reassurance.

But the plane waited on the tarmac for almost an hour while my tension mounted even higher. Then the captain made an announcement: 'We are sorry for the delay; there seems to be a problem with a passenger's immigration papers, but we hope to be taking off shortly.'

My heart was in my mouth. Over and over I rehearsed the words that I would say to any Egyptian official that came for Yasmeen: 'What is your name? Do you have a court order? On whose authority are you taking my daughter away?' I was prepared to fight physically for her if I had to.

I sat pretending to read a newspaper, hoping that Yasmeen wouldn't notice how the paper was trembling. And then I heard these wonderful words, from the captain to the cabin crew: 'Doors to automatic.' We were off!

A while later, when I was sure we were safe, I wrote a note to the captain to tell him that he was flying Yasmeen home after fourteen months of separation from her mother and her country. The captain came to greet us, congratulating me with a bottle of champagne and giving Yasmeen a 'Biggles' teddy bear. The cabin crew were delighted for us too, having read of our case in the papers. It was wonderful to feel so cosseted and cared for, after so many months of insecurity and fear.

But my joy at leaving Egypt with Yasmeen was clouded by thoughts of the two sweetest boys ever created – boys that we were leaving behind.

'Don't cry Mummy!' said Yasmeen. 'We'll get them back.'

As we flew over the pyramids towards England, I laughed and I cried, and my tears were tears of relief, joy – and deep, deep sadness.

Sawy and Sammie . . . as I
remember them

Happier days – two pictures from our life before the divorce. Abdel-Salam holds Sawy.

Abdel-Salam's parents, the children's Egyptian grandparents.

In the hospital after the stabbing.

Headline reads: This English woman is between life and
death. She tried to kidnap her children, and the father of her
Egyptian ex-husband stabbed her"

● ١٩٩٠/١٢/١٢

◌● أخبار الحوادث والقضايا ●◌

هذه الانجليزية بين الحياة والموت

حاولت خطف أطفالها .. فطعنها والد مطلقها المصري

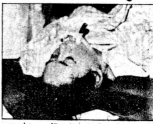

الأم الانجليزية: هبة الله .. كادت تلقى مصرعها بسبب
محاولتها استرداد اطفالها الثلاثة ● تصوير: محمد رجب ●

كتب رشاد كامل

سرقوا مدارس الجيزة !

كتب محيى عبدالرحمن

للمرة الثانية : منع أحمد ناصر من دخول نقابة المحامين

كتب : شريف خفاجى

المدعى العام الاشتراكي يقرر
صرف ٢ مليون جنيه من السبت القادم
لضحايا «بشرى معوض»

كتبت ايمان راشد

تعطل المترو
فأغمى على الركاب

ابحث مع الشرطة

مدمن يحرق

The front page of an Egyptian newspaper on the day after the
stabbing. The picture was captioned: This English woman is
between life and death. She tried to kidnap her children and the
father of her Egyptian ex-husband stabbed her.

Dear Baddy   1990 20 12

    you know how much Ilove you and care about you you are my only

      Father and I am so so sorry that when you came to the EMᴰBAᵛSY

         and called out my name and I did not come to you and any way ᵀI

            will never come home back home again becouseI will never have

               the time I hade with your father again You dont know what

                  YOU R father did to my mother he stabed her In her stpmach

      and in her back and when he did it in her stomacʰh he LENT on the knife

      andI dont think that he has got a HEARᵀT and when you came to the

      Embassy and called out my name the women that I was with was my auntie

      QWEEnNY .

And do you think that i am stupid to come and live with you again

Ha ha ha ha ha.

      your joking.

            Lots of horrible nights and wishes

                 from ⟨signature⟩

A bitter letter from Yasmeen to her father written while we
stayed in the Embassy after the knife attack. Yasmeen still misses
her brothers and father.

RAFFLE TO WIN CHILDREN BACK

Help recover children kidnapped from this country illegally. Your support is needed to fight in courts in the country where the children are hostages.

Tickets are £1 per strip to win a hamper, to save TINY HOSTAGES.

The Govt. are doing nothing to rescue Abducted British Children... the worst form of Child Abuse ... YOU CAN! PLEASE help rescue these British Children.

Left: A poster I made to publicize my situation which I used at local events and in pubs to raise money and support.

Below: Yasmeen and I with Anne Diamond and Esther Rantzen on *Hearts of Gold.* I eventually sold the car I won to raise money.

A picture Sawy gave me on one of my access visits in Cairo. He explained his picture to me: 'That's me and that's an aeroplane and I want to get on the plane and fly home to you, Mummy.' When grandmother learned what he'd said she laughed, saying that the picture showed Sawy's ambition to be a soldier in the Egyptian army.

Yasmeen drew me a picture, too. It says, 'Dear Mother Happy Day. I love you. Yasmeen xx'

British journalists Harry Arnold and Roger Alan took Yasmeen to the Pyramids while I was filming *First Sight* in Cairo. Yasmeen adores them both and the feeling is mutual.

Keeping my story in the headlines: TV crews from Sky and Thames News watch as I try to get the attention of Mrs Suzanne Mubarak, wife of the Egyptian President, outside the Embassy in London. Yasmeen was totally bored throughout.

Part Two

Chapter Seven

I was born in south London and grew up on Livingstone Road in Thornton Heath. I had one elder brother (David), two older sisters (Kath and Queenie), plus a younger brother, Christopher. My father had a garage around the corner where he repaired damaged cars, and my mother devoted her life to looking after my Dad and her children.

We spent many sunny days as a family before my mother became ill, and I relished the attention that she gave me in those days. I remember prancing about the back garden while my parents lazed on the grass. I remember my Mum saying to my Dad: 'That girl's got a beautiful figure.' It made me prance even more.

In those days we children would hear Mum and Dad coming home from the pub down the road and we listened gleefully as Dad pushed Mum on the swing in the garden. We knew when Mum had had more than one port and lemon because she would giggle like a young girl.

Our neighbours were two retired ladies, Auntie Bertha and Auntie Reine, whom I loved very much and who had a major influence on my life. My 'Aunties' taught me how to knit and how to make tea 'properly'. Auntie Reine also taught me French and the importance of not allowing boys to 'interfere with' me.

The house they lived in belonged to a missionary who had brought back umpteen treasures and ornaments from around the world. There was a family of carved wooden elephants from India, and a palm tree complete with a monkey climbing to eat the dates. Auntie Reine's and Auntie Bertha's house was a treasure trove which contained enticing secrets from far-away places, and it was there as a small child that I developed a lasting fascination with other cultures.

And then Mum became ill and the atmosphere of my home changed. I was eight at the time; Christopher was four; Kath was twelve and Queenie was thirteen. My eldest brother David had already left home to join the army. Our mother was ill for a long time and she used to drag her leg as she walked. No one knew the reason why, and she just got on with life. My vague memories of my mother are of a woman who constantly smiled, despite everything.

Our lav had been an outside one until my Dad incorporated it into the kitchen by knocking a wall down and making a connecting door. Mum was delighted, but one day as she was coming out of the lav, she caught her foot on a shallow step just inside the door and screamed in pain. I was in bed upstairs, but when I heard her scream I rushed downstairs with Christopher and my sisters. Queenie was sent to fetch Dad from the garage and to call the doctor.

That day was the beginning of a downhill slide for my Mum. We all congregated in the back room, Mum sitting on the sofa with her bad leg sticking straight out in front of her. I'll never forget that I accidentally knocked her leg, and she screamed in pain. When the doctor eventually came, he diagnosed a slipped disc and told her to lie down on a hard surface. Dad took the living-room door off its hinges and Mum was forced to sleep on it. She slept in the living room, but she was hardly able to move and my brother Chrissy and I ran riot. We spent a good deal of our time at Dad's garage, fashioning left-over 'filler' into different shapes.

My mother returned from a spell in hospital with the news that she had a fractured femur. In fact, she also had cancer, but this had not been diagnosed. It still makes me angry that she never got the care that she deserved – and, perhaps unfairly, that my father never made sure she was properly looked after.

They gave my mother a caliper which was supposed to help her walk again. I would run home from school as soon as I could every day to see if Mum was any better. I imagined her wearing her caliper and going for walks with me, but she found it too painful to wear the caliper. Then a wheelchair was brought to the house and Mum promised me that as soon as she was a bit better, I could push her down the road in her wheelchair.

I rushed home from school willing Mum to be better so that I could push her out into the fresh air, but every day she would say to me, 'Not today, love. Soon.' That was another dream that never came true. I began to lose hope that life would ever get back to normal. I was losing my mother and my security at much the same age as my son Sawy lost his, a fact that has made me doubly determined to rescue my children.

Then one day I went to see Dad at his garage on the way home from school. He said 'Go into the office. There is a surprise for you on the desk.' In a small cardboard box I found a tiny fluffy chick which I promptly named Suzy.

I took Suzy straight home to meet Mum, thinking that the chick would cheer her as much as she had cheered me. At home I opened the box and tipped the contents on to Mum's bed. But even the tiny movements that Suzy made on the blankets caused my mother agony and I realized just how much pain my mother was suffering.

Although she had been ill for a long time, we were not

prepared in any way for her death. One night I woke up and looked out of my bedroom window to see a coffin being brought into the house. I went on to the landing and called downstairs to my sisters: 'I saw a coffin, is Mum dead?' Queenie told me Mum wasn't dead but that she had gone to the hospital and the wooden box was to take her clothes.

I lay listening to the extraordinary quiet that had taken over our home, and when all was silent, I went downstairs to Mum's room. She was in bed with a sheet over her head. I uncovered her head. She was dead. There were no angels and nothing beautiful about my mother's death; just an overwhelming sense of loss.

Dad did his very best to care for his children in his own way after Mum died. One day, a man came from the school board and told him that his children were entitled to free school meals. But he would have none of it and shouted, 'I don't take charity', sending the man packing.

My father was a true craftsman in metal: he could mend and weld anything and to me he seemed a wizard of improvisation. He often said to me, 'Do what you want, not what other people tell you to do,' and the idea that I should always achieve my own aims in life made a lasting impression on me.

But after my mother died, my family experienced some very hard times and I learned the awful consequences of poverty at an early age. At times we did not even have lino on our floors, and my father was arrested for non-payment of taxes.

The day that the policeman came to take Dad away, Dad was cooking our supper on a coal fire in the back room because the electricity and gas had been cut off. It was a hot July day and the policeman removed his hat because of the heat in the room as he spoke to Dad. My father's behaviour was very humble indeed and I remember that I hated all that was happening.

My brother David wasn't at home very much. He never saw eye to eye with my father, and when he did come home, they would have terrifying fist fights. My mother used to break these up, but after her death there was no one to stop the violence. David kicked a big hole in the living-room door one day and Dad responded by cracking him over the head with a dining-room chair. Tension and trauma filled the house.

It must have been terrible for my father to have to cope with us children while he was grieving for his wife. Sometimes I would catch him staring at me with a sad look in his eyes. I knew that it was because I reminded him so much of Mum.

Kath was my protector and surrogate mother after Mum died, but she couldn't always be there, and when she wasn't I would turn to my Aunties next door. They meant very much to me and I loved them dearly. My brother Chris and I also had lovely cosy times together when just he and I were at home. Dad often went for a drink in the pub at the end of the road, and Chris and I would glue ourselves into the armchairs by the fire to watch TV and stuff ourselves with crisps and chocolate.

I hated school after Mum died. The day after she died, the headmistress told the entire school about my Mum's death during assembly. Every girl turned to stare at me and I felt terribly self-conscious. After that I would hear girls whispering loudly to each other in the school playground: 'That girl's mum is dead!' It was as if I had some awful disease. My best friends avoided me; they probably didn't know what to say.

Sometimes, on the way home from school, I would wonder if I had imagined my mother's death. Maybe it was a cruel joke that someone was playing on me. I would daydream that Mum was really still alive and waiting at home for me. Certainly her death had hit me at a vulnerable age and I feel that it left me with a lasting sense of insecurity.

When I grew older, friends remarked upon the fact that I was never without a boyfriend; as soon as one relationship ended, another began. I think that was because I felt painfully unloved unless I had someone to be with. It may also be that at a deep level, I was eventually attracted to and married an Egyptian man because his strict and patriarchal culture provided a kind of security – although, as a Western woman, another part of me fought against it continually.

A while after Mum died, I began ballet lessons. I had a flair for ballet and it became my obsession, taking up most of my time – and quite a lot of Dad's money. Kath always stood by me, and she supported me whenever I had to argue with Dad for ten shillings to pay for ballet lessons. God knows where she got the money from, but Kath also took me to London to see the ballet several times, and I was completely spellbound.

We also had wonderful days when we would go up to buy new ballet shoes from Freed's in London. The most exciting part of the day was trying on and buying the ballet shoes, but we also went to Trafalgar Square and to Swan and Edgar where we tried on clothes. We knew that we could never afford them, but it was fun to daydream.

I practised and practised my ballet exercises, becoming so proficient that my teacher recommended me to apply for a scholarship to enter the Ballet Rambert. But about a month before the scholarship examination I became seriously ill with rheumatic fever.

I was in hospital for several weeks, having daily, painful injections, and I would stare wistfully out of the window to see people walking on the streets of Croydon. I felt as if I was in prison. But on the day that I left hospital, Kath came to collect me with a brand-new mustard-coloured pinafore dress for me to put on.

I couldn't wait to get out of the hospital and to skip and run again. But as soon as I began to run, Kath would stop me; the doctor had told her that strenuous exercise – including ballet – was 'bad for my heart'. It wasn't long before the rules were relaxed and I was allowed to run about again, but with ballet, another important part of my life had disappeared. I felt that life had cheated me again.

As I grew older I became closer and closer to Kath and quite distant from Chris. Spoiled by our Dad to compensate for Mum's death, Chris's behaviour left a lot to be desired. Queenie had by now left school, was working in an office near our home and was going out with boys after work.

Kath was my idol because she was so clever and so serious compared to me. She was also 'arty' and was studying hard to enter teacher training college. We were both still at Ecclesbourne Secondary School, a forty-minute walk from home. It was terrible in the winter because Kath and I didn't have proper winter coats.

When I was thirteen, Queenie got married and had her first baby. She and her husband moved into an unfurnished flat in Norwood and I visited her as often as I could. I loved Queenie's new home and could hardly wait to be old enough to move out of Livingstone Road myself.

I was fed up with arguments at home, fed up with having to fight for a place to sit because the sofa was broken in several places. All in all my childhood had been a bit of a struggle. We hadn't had a very good time of it at home, but now I could see the light at the end of the tunnel.

It is hardly a wonder, then, that I was in such a rush to get married and to make my own home. One night when I was only fifteen I went to a dance in a Croydon pub hall. It was packed with people with Indian and Caribbean backgrounds; I was the only white girl present. The lead singer in the band was a man in green satin bell bottom trousers and a gaudy waistcoat.

His name was George and he sang to me personally, adding my name to the lyrics. I was immediately besotted and accepted his invitation to go to the next dance. My father forbade me to see 'that black man' again, but in the end he relented and agreed to our marriage. That was probably because I told Dad that if he wouldn't agree I would run away fom home anyway. Poor Dad.

I married George on 21 November 1971. By that time I had left school and was working in a boutique in Croydon. Not surprisingly, our marriage didn't last long. I wanted to go out and have a good time, while George just wanted me to take care of him at home. Looking back, it's quite clear to me that I married to escape my childhood home.

Chapter Eight

For the next six years, home was a variety of London flats while I worked mostly as a freelance demonstrator in exhibitions (such as the Ideal Home Exhibition) up and down the country. It was comparatively well-paid work, and I enjoyed my life and my annual holidays in Tunisia, Cyprus or Athens.

And as my best friend Jill pointed out, I was never without a boyfriend, hating the sense of being unwanted. One of these boyfriends was Italian, and he took me to a nightclub called Thursdays on Kensington High Street. When our relationship ended, I went again to Thursdays with my friend Jill, and began going out with the cocktail barman, an Egyptian called Mohammed Taha.

It was Mohammed Taha who introduced Jill and me to Abdel-Salam Ahmed, a man who was to become my husband and the father of my three children. Abdel-Salam was introduced to me as Mohammed's cousin, but while Mohammed was tall, slim and attractive, Abdel-Salam was very much shorter and fatter.

'No!' Jill whispered. 'He's not Mohammed's cousin! I don't believe it!' Mohammed creased up laughing and said, 'He is a farmer!' I couldn't see the joke. Why was Abdel-Salam such a figure of fun? What was so funny about being a farmer? I later realized that his Cairo friends thought of Abdel as an unsophisticated peasant because his family came from a village and worked the land. (I was later to discover just how poor his family was, even by Egyptian standards.)

Abdel-Salam didn't waste much time with Jill and me after we had given him such short shrift. Instead he went off to gossip with other Egyptian men who worked at Thursdays. But I was to see plenty of Abdel-Salam in the coming months.

Mohammed Taha lived in one of several large airy bedsits in a house off Westbourne Grove where various other Egyptian friends also lived. Abdel-Salam was often part of the crowd when I visited Mohammed, and as I listened to them talking, I began to get an insight into the Egyptian way of thinking. Conversation often revolved around money – or the lack of it. There was also a lot of concern about visas and entry permits, and the difficulties faced by illegal immigrants. In time I came to understand that a visa and a job in England represented the pinnacle of success to these young men who had little chance of a decent income back home.

In Cairo few of them could hope to earn enough to set up home away from their parents. Without such a home, they could not marry. And for most Egyptian girls, sex before marriage was out of the question. Whereas to many Egyptians, the West is viewed with suspicion and deemed decadent, some of Abdel's crowd seemed to think that an English girlfriend was herself a passport to good fortune.

I noticed again that Abdel-Salam was rather a figure of fun among his friends. But he was an extraordinarily jovial person, always laughing, even when the joke was on him.

My relationship with Mohammed Taha ended on a sour note when I returned from a week's holiday in Athens to find that my boyfriend didn't want to see me any more. He wouldn't tell me so; he just ignored my calls.

I felt that this was very cowardly of him and on several occasions I went to the house off Westbourne Grove wanting to face him. It was always Abdel-Salam who opened the door to me and who told me that Mohammed was not at home (although I knew very well that he was).

Then one day I walked into a fish and chip shop in Westbourne Grove and found Abdel-Salam working there. By now his face had become familiar to me, and we chatted for a while. When Abdel-Salam asked me out to dinner the following night, I was surprised to find myself accepting his invitation. The man that I had at first found so unappealing was behaving like a friend, and it was a good feeling, almost like a truce.

Abdel-Salam met me at Bayswater tube station the next evening. He was all dressed up for dinner, and we went to a kebab house in Westbourne Grove. Abdel-Salam knew the restaurant owner and the staff who were all very chatty and friendly with him. I began to see that my view of Abdel-Salam had been coloured by the teasing of Mohammed and his friends, and I realized that I hardly knew him.

He seemed to be really interested in me as a person and I found it easy to open up to him. Slowly, we began to learn about each other. He was quietly spoken and attentive, and he had a wonderful sense of humour. It was turning into a surprisingly relaxed and enjoyable evening. Abdel-Salam asked me about my family, wanting to know how many brothers and sisters I had and what my father did for a living. He also told me about his family in Egypt. His parents and his brother Gamal now lived in Cairo, but the family originally came from a small village called Sukaria in the county of Minofia, sixty kilometres from Cairo.

Abdel-Salam explained the history of his family and told me about those who still lived in the village. The first member of his family to settle in Sukaria was Ahmed El-Sawy who had escaped compulsory labour building the

Suez Canal (in the 1860s) and had sought refuge there.

Abdel-Salam's story was colourful and fascinating, and slowly I found myself feeling a strong attraction towards him. First, he became a friend, but then friendship developed into romance. It seemed to me at the time that he was a simple man with simple ambitions: he told me that what he wanted more than anything was to lead a peaceful life with a loyal partner. I knew that he was a hard-working man, and I also thought that he was down-to-earth and honest.

Looking back on our relationship, I see that there are other reasons why we got together. After the early loss of my mother and a rather turbulent childhood, I had grown into an insecure young woman. Abdel, with his clear, traditional values, offered security to me.

As for Abdel-Salam, although I didn't know it at the time, he was working illegally in the UK. In retrospect I've realized that his motive in going out with me was to get a visa and a resident's permit.

In November 1978, Abdel-Salam told me that his father had ordered him home to Cairo to complete his studies in accountancy. He had written back to his parents telling them that he would be returning to Cairo soon – with his new wife. I was horrified that he had lied to his parents, but he said: 'You will marry me in Egypt and I will treat you like a Queen. I will make you the happiest woman on Earth.' Abdel assured me that we would be warmly welcomed into his family home in Cairo as man and wife. He argued that it was a small fib to tell them that we were already married: if I would agree to be his wife then we would be partners 'in God's eyes'.

We flew to Cairo a month later, planning to stay there

for six months before returning to the UK. I was puzzled when Abdel-Salam offered the immigration officer a piece of paper from the Egyptian Embassy instead of a passport, but he told me that his passport had gone missing and this was an emergency travel document. Not knowing that he had stayed illegally in Britain, I thought no more of it.

Abdel-Salam's father, Mohammed El-Sawy, and his brother Gamal were waiting for us at the airport. His father spoke no English at all, but Gamal spoke a little and in the black-and-white taxi that belonged to Mohammed El-Sawy we managed a halting conversation. But I didn't really want to talk: I wanted to look at the new sights all around me, the beautiful white buildings and the tree-lined avenues.

Soon the avenues were becoming narrower, and definitely dirtier. We were driving in a swerving, hooting, careering stream of traffic which reminded me of bumper cars at an English fairground. Children sat close against the windscreens on their mothers' laps in the front passenger seats, without seat belts. I saw buses so crammed with passengers that men hung from their roofs and windows, and in among the traffic I caught a glimpse of a donkey and cart piled impossibly high.

Some of the people thronging the pavements wore rather drab western style clothes. Others wore traditional long robes and headscarves, but the women were all well covered without a trace of bare arm or leg. When the traffic was stopped at lights by whistle-blowing policemen, young beggars, some with limbs missing, threaded their way through the cars to appeal for money. I had not been prepared for this.

And then we were driving through an area that looked half demolished. Great potholes cratered the road surface while derelict buildings and piles of rubble and rubbish were on either side. I thought at first that Abdel-Salam's father was taking a short cut, and so I got a serious shock when the car stopped outside a building that looked as if it should have been condemned as unsafe.

I followed Abdel-Salam and his father up a winding staircase to the very top of the building. Abdel-Salam had told me that his family were poor, but I wasn't prepared for the level of poverty that I now encountered. I was led into a small room and was horrified at the scene before me. There was a double bed and an uncomfortable-looking sofa against one wall. On the bed was Abdel-Salam's other brother El-Sawy. Abdel-Salam had never mentioned this brother, who seemed to be having some kind of fit. Abdel-Salam's mother was restraining him, but she let go of El-Sawy in order to kiss Abdel who had been away for eighteen months.

As soon as El-Sawy was released, he held out his hand and asked me for something, over and over again. I saw that he was mentally handicapped and his parents hurriedly explained that he had been kidnapped when he was sixteen and used as a beggar for a year by his kidnappers. A year later he had been abandoned in a cemetery, wearing rags, but he had never lost the habit of begging.

The family home consisted of two rooms, both with beds in, one of which doubled as a kitchen. Abdel-Salam's mother did all of the cooking on a kerosene-fuelled burner such as I had only seen on camping holidays until then. There was a communal toilet, shared by five other families, and the sole source of water was a single tap beside the lavatory. There was no bath and no shower – other than that afforded by the one cold tap.

I was completely shocked by what I saw, and my mind was reeling. I whispered in a panicky voice to Abdel-Salam: 'Where are we going to sleep?' I hoped fervently that I wasn't expected to sleep with his mother! Fortunately, he told me that we were to be given the privacy of one room together. His parents must have known that we were 'living in sin' – this was two months before our marriage – but they swept this fact under the carpet. It was more important to them that their son, in forming a liaison with me, was on the verge of getting that precious British visa.

Abdel-Salam's mother brought in mountains of food that she had prepared for her eldest son's homecoming, and we ate, sitting cross-legged on the floor, from a low round table. I had no appetite, but Abdel-Salam urged me to tuck in, warning that his mother would be very offended if I didn't eat.

I tentatively used my first words of Arabic, saying 'Shokran!' (thank you) to my future mother-in-law for the food she had prepared. But as hard as I tried, I couldn't feel at ease. Finally, his family went to bed and Abdel-Salam and I had some precious time alone to talk privately.

He apologized for not telling me about El-Sawy: he had been ashamed and too afraid to tell me. El-Sawy had been very ill as a child, and since the age of three he had been paralysed on one side and had suffered fits. I wondered, not for the first time, about the availability of health care in Egypt.

A day that had begun full of excitement and promise had ended in total disappointment. I felt numb with shock, but Abdel-Salam assured me that things would look better in the morning.

The next morning certainly was brighter, but only in terms of the sunshine which highlighted the dirt and poverty of Sharabiya, the notorious slum district where Abdel-Salam's relatives lived.

The day was spent in a round of visits to friends and neighbours. Unable to speak Arabic, I felt very left out. Abdel-Salam's mother had the strange idea that if she shouted loud enough in my ear, I would understand her.

Many people that we visited wanted to touch my hair and my clothes which I found acutely embarrassing. I spent much of that day staring at my shoes like a child, terrified of catching someone's eye lest they start chattering to me in Arabic. I had to work hard to stop myself from crying.

I realized how much I had taken for granted back home in the UK and vaguely wondered if this experience was some kind of lesson for me. The strain was enormous, but I told myself that I had to make the best of what I had, and that somehow Abdel-Salam and I would make it through and be happy.

Abdel-Salam was also feeling the strain: three days after we arrived in Cairo I found him sobbing uncontrollably on the small balcony of the living room. As he poured out his feelings of despair and disappointment, I couldn't help but feel sorry for him. 'What have I done?' he sobbed. 'How could I bring you to this? I can't live like this any more, so how can I expect you to?' In his eighteen months in London, Abdel-Salam had all but forgotten the poverty that he had left behind in Sharabiya.

We discussed our feelings and fears frankly, and Abdel-Salam told me that he knew he would not be able to make a living for us in Cairo. We both agreed that we should go back to London as soon as he had finished his studies at the University. In the meantime, we would look for our own flat.

Abdel-Salam's father, who by day worked as a driver for a government ministry in central Cairo, was by night a taxi driver. His black-and-white taxi had been bought with money sent by Abdel-Salam from London, and now we set out in the taxi to search for a cheap but decent apartment for Abdel-Salam and me.

But Abdel-Salam's father and I had very different ideas about the kind of place we were looking for. He drove us to see a string of apartments that were cheap but utterly filthy and run down. Abdel-Salam was losing his patience as he explained yet again to his father why I refused to live in such a place.

We agreed to take a break before we all went crazy and we went to visit Abdel-Salam's aunt who lived in Pyramids Street in Giza – a much better district than Sharabiya. The hedges on the street's grassy central reserve were clipped into pyramid shapes, and they extended all the way up to the Pyramids. I was enchanted.

We were warmly welcomed by Abdel-Salam's aunt and her little boy, Magdi. I was quite impressed by her spacious home (she had her own servant) but it was impossible to ignore the dirt of the place. I found myself wishing that I could ask for a bucket and a mop to clean it up.

After all the chit-chat and many 'how are yous?' were over, Aunty told us that there was an empty apartment in a building just over the road, and she went to talk to the caretaker. After what seemed like hours of waiting, she was back, huffing and puffing and fanning herself on the sofa while we waited for her news.

She told us that the apartment was still empty and the price was £10 a month. Despite Abdel-Salam's father's reservations about the price, we were very excited at the prospect and set off to see it straight away. It was in a small, two-storey block with an ornate wrought-iron door in the centre. Inside, its walls were pale green and very grubby, but I knew I could brighten them up, and there was a wooden-framed three-piece suite that would be gorgeous after I had re-covered the cushions. All that was needed to improve the bathroom was some bleach and scouring powder.

I could imagine Abdel-Salam and me walking around our home, happy together. I pictured it decorated with vases of flowers; the aromas of cooking wafting from the kitchen – and mornings of opening the shutters to flood the rooms with brilliant sunlight. But more than anything, I longed for the bliss of privacy from his parents.

We all went into the living room to discuss the minutest details: even the simplest transaction is made complicated in Egypt. The caretaker, Fathi, had lively intelligent eyes and spoke a little English and with him we discussed the fairness of the price, the condition of the apartment and the inventory of the apartment – down to the last teaspoon.

As we signed our contract, Fathi's wife Ridda knocked on the door. She was very friendly and invited us all to tea in their home on the ground floor. Ridda then pampered us with cola, tea, homemade cakes and biscuits followed by freshly made lemonade, until Fathi handed over the key to our new home.

Abdel-Salam and I agreed to collect our belongings from Sharabiya and move in immediately, but every time I thought that enough goodbyes had been said, I was told to sit down again. Since my arrival in Egypt I seemed to be spending all of my time sitting with my hands folded, waiting to get going. I was learning fast that it is the height of rudeness in Egypt not to shake hands with every person present and to spend time in greeting or saying goodbye to them.

Finally, we were on our way to collect our things from Sharabiya. I couldn't wait to be myself again, away from the scrutiny of Abdel-Salam's parents. I was tired of being the object of curiosity, ogled by all and sundry because I was 'Ag'nabiyya' (a foreign woman).

The family ate together in Sharabiya before Abdel-Salam

and I left their flat. His mother feigned disappointment about our move and hugged me tightly, saying, 'You are leaving me?' But I felt sure that she was resentful: in her eyes, I was guilty of taking her eldest son away from her. I didn't know it at the time but she had lost nine children in infancy. Could that have been one of the reasons why she later took away mine?

Our first night in our new home was bliss. We had no hot water because the butane gas bottle that fuelled the water heater was empty. There was a power failure that cut the electricity off for three hours. But it was heaven for us both as we wandered half-dressed around our home. I cooked a quick meal of scrambled eggs with feta cheese, so as not to waste a second of the pleasure that I felt in sitting with Abdel-Salam on our first night in our first real home.

Then our new neighbours knocked on our door and introduced themselves and Abdel-Salam and I played host. A party soon developed for all the residents of No. 32 Rameses the Second Street and children were sent out again and again for more Sport Cola from the tiny grocery shop opposite our apartment. And long after I felt that I couldn't stand another person trying to teach me the entire Arabic language in one evening, everyone went home.

It was finally time for Abdel-Salam and me to be alone, to go to bed and to make love. After we had made love we showered. It didn't matter that the water was cold and it didn't matter that we had no light. We stumbled about blissfully, and then slept happily as a unit.

The days and weeks that followed were packed full of life. Our home became a meeting-place for Abdel-Salam's friends, eager to see him after his return from London – and even more eager to see that he really had brought a British 'wife' home to Egypt with him. Abdel-Salam's brother Gamal was also a frequent caller, bringing with him any friends that he could in order to impress them with our relatively high standard of living. We didn't have much money – Abdel-Salam was studying and his father was subsidizing us – but the savings we had brought with us from London went a long way in Cairo.

Yet when the initial interest in us had waned, I found that I was being left alone in the flat more and more frequently. Abdel-Salam claimed that he was studying with friends because it was difficult to concentrate alone. Often he left home at around six in the evening and didn't return home until five or six in the morning. I was suspicious that there wasn't much studying going on because he always returned home 'stoned' from smoking hashish. But I put my fears on one side and concentrated on the positive side of our relationship. And I comforted myself with the knowledge that – back home in England – life would be very different.

I couldn't see why Abdel-Salam was completing his studies in accountancy when we both knew that he would be working in catering in the UK. Any degree that he was awarded in Egypt would not be valid in England, but he explained time and time again that it was shameful for anyone in Egypt not to achieve their goal in education.

Abdel-Salam's father had lent us the family TV set because I was often alone in the apartment, and I used it as my tutor in Arabic. I would listen and write down the words which I heard repeated often. When Abdel-Salam came home, I would ask him for a translation. One word which I heard constantly on an Egyptian soap-opera was 'Maz-mazeel', which sounded attractively oriental. Abdel-Salam laughed when I asked him what it meant: it was the Egyptian way of saying 'Mademoiselle'.

Abdel-Salam's father would also visit me when his son was out, to teach me the Arabic language. We got along better when we were alone, without an audience for our battles. I learned the Arabic alphabet from him and gradually my Arabic improved.

Egyptian food was another hurdle. I desperately wanted to do my best and to provide hospitality to my guests, but my cooker – with its feeble gas jets – was not up to the task. I tried very hard to make the dishes that I had made so easily in London, but success evaded me in my Cairo kitchen.

On one occasion, Abdel-Salam's father popped in to see us. Abdel-Salam and I were about to eat, so his father was invited to join us. I had spent three days searching the shops for a cheddar-type cheese with which to make macaroni cheese, and I thought that I had finally managed it. The dish looked good when I took it out of the oven, but it tasted horrible and even I lost my enthusiasm after a few mouthfuls. Abdel-Salam's father recited the traditional Muslim grace before starting to eat. Then he tried to eat the meal, but his disgust was obvious, and it was only seconds before he recited the grace to finish the meal: 'Al-Humdu lillah'.

Embarrassed, I hurriedly made tea for us all. While I was in the kitchen I heard my future father-in-law telling his son that it would be a good idea for his mother to come around every Friday so that she could teach me to cook. He was apparently worried that his son would die of hunger if left to me. As I served the tea, I said to Abdel-Salam, 'Please tell your father that I am really sorry the meal was not good. And please tell him that I do know how to cook, but everything is so different here.' But Mohammed El-Sawy was not convinced and insisted that he and his wife spend every Friday with me. I knew that he felt I needed not only his wife's guidance in the kitchen, but his advice on how to conduct my life. He believed that, as a European, I was spoiled and over-privileged compared with members of his own family. His mission was to somehow retrain me in order to change me and make me a better wife to his son.

And so it was that one of the first words that I learned in Arabic was 'Alibee' (stir it). Abdel-Salam's mother used this word again and again during her cooking lessons. I did a lot of stirring in those days, patiently listening to and watching her. I learned a great deal about Abdel-Salam's mother too, and about the expectations of Egyptian women.

She had been brought up to do whatever her husband told her without question. As a girl in an Egyptian village she must have learned from babyhood that her worth was less than that of any male. She came from a culture in which males are always treated as superior beings to females. Egyptian girls of her background, apart from going through the pain and trauma of circumcision at an early age, generally get less freedom, less respect, less education – even less food – than their brothers.

Above all, Egyptian women are expected to obey men, and it was clear that my mother-in-law thought that I was no exception. But her attitudes were quite alien to me and I had no wish to emulate her subservient behaviour.

Yet still I felt confident that Abdel-Salam and I could be happy together. In the early days, our marriage did feel good, cosy and secure. I was at the age where I believed I could change the world, so the prospect of bridging the cultural gap between myself and my husband seemed a small problem.

And after all, Abdel-Salam was from a younger generation. Surely he would not treat me the way his father treated his mother? Surely, for us, things would be different?

Chapter Nine

In January 1979, Abdel-Salam and I made arrangements for our wedding. Before we could be married according to British law, we had to be married according to Egyptian law. There was a lot of red tape to deal with, but eventually, on 18 January, we were married at a Cairo register office in the presence of Abdel-Salam's father. I don't know why his mother chose not to come. There was no elaborate reception, simply a meal at his parents' home in Sharabiya, and I was aware that the whole occasion was very low key compared with most Egyptian weddings. I assume now that his mother saw it as no more than a formality on the way to her son's visa.

Then on 28 February 1979, we were married according to British law in the Consular Section of the British Embassy. It was all very formal. The Consul's desk was draped with a Union Jack and there was a large framed photograph of the Queen on the wall behind. We didn't have enough money for a white wedding dress, but I was in heaven because I was now truly Abdel-Salam's wife.

His old friends Mohammed Hanafy and Osairma Taha were our witnesses. Osairma had to keep his head down for the whole wedding ceremony because he had recently had a run-in with the British Pro-Consul – who was acting as a witness – when he had been refused an entry permit to the UK. Abdel-Salam made both our witnesses giggle when he got his words wrong: instead of reciting 'Holy Matrimony' after the Consul, he said 'Much Money'.

Soon my husband and I left the Embassy arm in arm, feeling very proud and respectable. With our two friends we set off to visit the Pyramids, where we celebrated our union by eating Egyptian bean sandwiches washed down with Sport Cola. And then Abdel-Salam and I went home to make legal love until the party later that night.

All of Abdel's friends came to the party at his Aunt's house in Pyramids Street, as well as his immediate family. Two uncles came from the village in Minofia, wearing traditional Arab dress. To my surprise, my father-in-law had rolled no less than twenty hashish cigarettes for our guests and had even bought bottles of alcohol. (Drinking alcohol was technically against my new relatives' religion, but they did drink on occasion.)

Our music centre had been brought over from our flat, and it wasn't long before the living room resembled a London disco. Then Abdel-Salam's father and his two brothers danced a traditional stick dance, waving sticks over their heads in an imitation battle. I was enthralled, but to my disappointment, Abdel-Salam became acutely embarrassed, revealing that he was ashamed of his origins. What seemed so romantic to me as a Westerner served only to remind him of the 'peasant' background which he wished so fervently to escape.

Two days after our (British) wedding, Abdel-Salam and I went back to the Embassy to apply for a permit for my husband to enter the UK. I was confident that we would have no problems: wasn't he after all my husband now?

The visa section was crammed with Egyptians desperate to escape the poverty and chaos of Cairo, and a long tangle of people were queuing for application forms. Abdel-Salam told me to push straight to the front: he said that as a woman, I was not expected to queue with men. Queue-jumping is an art form in Egypt and one that I quickly learned to master: I held my British passport aloft while Abdel-Salam shoved me from behind, ordering people out of the way.

We had a long wait, but at last we heard the words over the tannoy: 'Abdel-Salam Ahmed. Baab sitta. (Door six).' The visa officer looked at us stony-faced and told us that just because Abdel-Salam was my husband, he had no automatic right to entry to the UK. I was surprised and disappointed, but I still didn't realize what a battle we had ahead of us in getting Abdel-Salam's visa.

In the meantime I kept busy by keeping our flat in an immaculate condition and decorating it to my own stand-ards. After I had painted the walls, I proudly hung up the posters that I had brought with me from London. One was a Pre-Raphaelite picture of Narcissus with nymphs, naked in a pool of water.

My father-in-law was horrified when he saw them and told his son that pictures of nudes were not appreciated in Egypt. He insisted that they be removed immediately. I was furious, but Abdel-Salam suggested we took them down and replace them after his father had left. But I stuck to my guns: were we going to take them down every time that he came round?

My father-in-law's response was angrily to rip my posters from the wall before he left in a storm. I was in tears for hours as Abdel-Salam tried to explain why his father had behaved that way. He blamed his father's age, his upbring-ing, his village background – but I felt that it was time his father made a few allowances for *my* background and culture too. I carefully taped the pieces of the posters back together, and rehung them.

That was one of many arguments with my father-in-law. Over the coming months I was forced to listen to him telling me about how the British had destroyed Egypt during their seventy-year occupation. He was adamant that the British had set Egypt back by hundreds of years and he made certain that – as a British citizen – I shouldered my share of the blame.

In February we went to Sukaria, the village where Abdel-Salam was born. Abdel-Salam's parents drove us there in the black-and-white taxi, accompanied by his brother El-Sawy. The scenery changed dramatically as we drove towards Sukaria: it was wonderful to see green fields and to breathe the sweet-smelling air of Minofia after the dry dust and sand that permeates Cairo.

As we drove along, my father-in-law told me that the county of Minofia was the most fertile in Egypt. Not only did it boast the best agricultural produce in Egypt, but it had produced President Sadat and Gamal Abdel Nasser too. By the roadside were vendors selling oranges from their family farms and my father-in-law stopped the car to buy some. They were so juicy that I ate a kilo of them during the rest of the journey to Sukaria – much to my in-laws' amusement.

I also saw women washing clothes in the stream along the way, and I saw a man, stark naked, having a good scrub. My mother-in-law turned my head away, not wanting me to see a man other than my husband without clothes on. The stream became narrower as we neared Sukaria and then we reached the entrance to the village, which was a gateway with the letters SUKARIA written across it. In years to come, my English-born children were to spend many months within the confines of that village.

My father-in-law negotiated the narrow track carefully (there are no paved roads in Sukaria) and we passed homes that were built of mud with open apertures for windows. I caught glimpses of women working in their homes and saw young children playing in the stream beneath a tiny wooden bridge. It was as if nothing had changed in the village for hundreds of years.

Abdel-Salam took the enchantment out of the scene by telling me that it was very dangerous for the children to play in the stream. He had done so as a child, against his parents' orders, and as a result had contracted a disease called bilharzia which occurs when tiny snail-like creatures living in streams penetrate the body and infect the kidneys. Bilharzia is a killer, and even when treated early, can still affect the health of the carrier into adulthood.

I hoped that Abdel-Salam's childhood home was not a tiny mud hut. Fortunately, it wasn't. It was a large mud hut. But I was still enchanted and excited, wanting to know everything about my husband's origins. The entire family were waiting for Abdel-Salam to arrive. Two uncles, their two wives, Abdel-Salam's grandmother and what seemed to be a whole primary-school's-worth of children were assembled to greet us. We were welcomed warmly, with kisses all round and at least twenty minutes of handshakes and 'how are yous'. People from all over the village had come to welcome back a son of Minofia.

El-Sawy, whose mental age was about three, became over-excited and started dribbling and then frothing at the mouth while frenziedly introducing me to people as his new sister. It seemed as if he were about to have another fit and his parents had to be firm with him and calm him down. Yet did his father really have to shout at him that he was the son of a dog while ordering him to take his pills immediately? I realized then that the pocket of El-Sawy's gown was full of pills that he administered to himself.

El-Sawy then spent most of the day sobbing in the corner, repeating over and over again, 'I am very sorry, father.' Then the women went to sit in one room while the men sat in another – with the exception of El-Sawy who was sitting with the women while shouting out his apology to his father in the next room.

I still spoke very little Arabic, and without my husband next to me I felt totally alien and uncomfortable. I couldn't understand a word said by the village women, who resorted to sign language, asking me again and again when I was going to have a baby. I didn't know how long we could keep up with these efforts and so I excused myself and went to look for my husband.

He was sitting with the men on the floor in another room. They were all smoking sheeshas (hubbly-bubbly pipes) and the smell of hashish was very pungent indeed. Abdel-Salam's face was as red as a beetroot and he couldn't stop laughing.

I was furious, and told him that I wanted to have a walk with him in the beautiful green fields all around us. He said 'in a minute' and I went back to wait in the room full of women. I waited an hour, and then went back to my husband and said that I was going to take a walk by myself. Abdel-Salam knew that I meant it, and so he hauled himself up, staggered into the room full of women and announced that I wanted to walk in the fields. All of the women got up to go with us.

'Can't we go alone, Abdel-Salam?' I asked him. He told me that they would think it very strange indeed and would be offended. So we all prepared to troop out together. Just then an old man arrived who clearly commanded respect and I got the impression that he was a village 'elder'. A chair was brought for him and I was told to wait a while longer for my walk.

I sat down again and a school friend of my husband's who spoke a little English made conversation with me. While we talked, the old man began shouting in Arabic and got up from his chair to brandish it in the air in a threatening manner. I asked my husband's friend what was going on, but he fobbed me off, saying he didn't understand.

And then I heard the old man shout 'Sharamouta!' I knew that the word meant prostitute and I knew that he was referring to me. Was it my clothes? I was wearing a conservative suit with a skirt that came well below the knee, but I pulled my skirt down even further. The men of the family led the old man away as he continued to shout that awful word. Insulted and angry, I burst into tears.

Abdel-Salam came to comfort me, lying that the old man had not been talking about me. And anyway, insisted my husband, he hadn't said 'sharamouta'; I had misheard. Then he took me for my walk around the village, but I could hardly see in front of me for the tears that filled my eyes. Abdel-Salam explained that most of the villagers had not even seen Cairo, let alone London, and so I should make allowances for them. But yet again, it seemed that no allowances were being made for me.

However, as we walked around the village together my spirits revived. I saw fields of cotton and of corn, and orange groves which intoxicated me with their perfume. Walking down a narrow, winding track, we came across a man hand-spinning cotton. I wanted to ask him about his ancient skill, but Abdel-Salam said he would be offended and think I was making fun of him.

My husband tried to cheer me by telling stories of his childhood. Once, when he was four, he was caught lying on top of a little girl in a field. The girl's mother had grabbed him and rubbed raw onions in his eyes to make him cry. I was horrified, but I was fast learning that things are done differently in the villages of Egypt.

My husband's father had also beaten him severely for his misdemeanour. Abdel-Salam had been so incensed that he had climbed up a high tree outside his home the next day, waiting for his father to return from work in the fields. He had thrown stones at his father – thinking his father wouldn't know where they were coming from – but after only a few stones his father looked up and ordered Abdel-Salam down from the tree. Abdel-Salam had been so terrified at the thought of a further beating that he fell out of the tree and hurt himself badly.

I was getting tired – it had been a long day – and so we walked back to the family home where a wonderful meal was waiting for us. We ate pitta bread, baked in a clay oven, and tiny, bullet-shaped cabbage leaves stuffed with rice, herbs and tomato sauce. And then we said goodbye to all of the family and began the hour and a half car journey back to Cairo.

When we arrived home, Abdel-Salam told me to put all of our clothes straight into soak in case they were carrying fleas from the village. As far as I was concerned, Sukaria had definitely lost its charm.

Chapter Ten

In February 1979 Kath wrote that she was coming to visit me in Cairo. I was delighted and I couldn't wait to see my sister and soul mate again. Before she had even boarded the plane to Cairo there were offers of marriage for her. Osairma Taha, who had been a witness at our wedding, had asked Abdel-Salam for my sister's hand in marriage – no doubt scenting another visa opportunity.

Kath arrived on 15 March, and I was determined that everything should be perfect for her. I had overlooked the fact that when she had met Abdel-Salam in London, she had made it clear that she didn't take to him. (This was not because of his race: she had liked my previous boyfriend, Mohammed Taha.)

Osairma drove us to the airport, and we went to the arrivals gate. It was crammed with waiting people and armed soldiers were posted at the immigration control points. I couldn't wait to see my sister's face, and as Abdel-Salam and Osairma examined the baggage coming out of arrivals, I saw Kath walking towards me. I ran towards her, calling her name as I ran. I was stopped briefly by the armed soldier but he waved me on with a smile. When I finally reached Kath and embraced her, there were cheers from behind me, as if I had scored a goal! The cheers became louder as my sister and I held each other tight. One of the nicest things about Egypt is the way its people share in each other's joy, rejoicing at seeing another's happiness.

And then I wanted to tell Kath everything. 'Take a

breath, girl!' she said as we drove through Cairo, 'we've got plenty of time.' Once we had welcomed her into our home, and she had given me all the latest news from home, the two of us went into the kitchen to make coffee. Kath said, 'I don't think that man [Osairma] likes me.' I told my incredulous sister that she couldn't be more wrong: 'Before you even left London, Kath, he was asking to marry you!' It was a long way from Croydon to Cairo.

The next day Abdel-Salam and I went with Kath and Osairma to the Pyramids and then to a café by the Nile. The Nile is an enchanting river and Egyptians say that, 'Anyone who drinks from the Nile must return to Egypt.' (As everyone who visits Egypt must drink water that comes from the Nile, it follows that anyone who visits Egypt will always return.)

Later that evening in our flat, Kath and Osairma were making plans to go sightseeing together the next day. Abdel-Salam called me into the bedroom for a private word. He explained to me that it is not done in Egypt for a woman to go out with a man alone, especially when she has only known him for a short time. He said that my sister ought to have a chaperone. Kath was very offended by this idea and accused Abdel-Salam of labelling her as a prostitute.

I could see both their points of view: he was trying to protect her, but she couldn't see why. The cultural divide between them was too wide to bridge. What should have been a delightful holiday was turning into a nightmare. How was I going to keep my husband *and* my sister happy?

Kath insisted on going out with Osairma that evening – without any chaperone – and arrived home late. While she was out, Abdel-Salam fretted about what the neighbours would think. When Kath came back, she announced that she and Osairma were going out again the next day — alone. There was an argument, Kath packed her clothes and said that she was going to book into a hotel. 'Let her go,' said Abdel-Salam.

I couldn't let her go. She was my sister, and she had brought me up as if she was my mother. Our love ran very deep. I explained all this to Abdel-Salam, but he would not relent. He insisted that my sister's behaviour in Egypt would reflect on me, and wasn't I his wife? I begged Kath not to leave, but between her stubbornness and Abdel-Salam's obstinacy, I had no chance of success.

In the end, I ran out of the house in tears while my husband followed me up Pyramids Street. I pleaded with him to be more understanding, and finally, he gave in. Kath could stay, but he wanted no part in her relationship with Osairma and his parents were not to know what was happening. I was distressed that my sister and my husband had set off on the wrong foot and I was very sad indeed when my sister flew home to London. But mingled with the sadness was a certain amount of relief that I would no longer have to act as a referee between my English sister and my Egyptian husband.

At about this time, I took a major step away from my London background by converting to Islam. I had previously been an agnostic, hating church as a child and convinced that what I heard there was no more than fairy stories.

I had however been attracted to Islam for some time. I had first heard the call to prayer when on holiday in Tunisia, and the fascination of that sound had stayed with me. In Egypt of course, with mosques on every street corner and the call to prayer pealing out five times a day, I was immersed in Islam and began to absorb it. While in Cairo in early 1979 I first read the Koran (in English translation), and I felt that I was reading history. This religion felt right for me and I asked Abdel-Salam how I could become a Muslim.

He told me that it was not necessary to go through any formalities: if I was a Muslim in my heart, that was enough for God. I was later to regret the fact that he deceived me on this: after abducting the children he told the Egyptian courts that I was a Christian not a Muslim. I did then get an official certificate to say that I was a Muslim, but as it was dated after the abduction, it failed to convince the Egyptian courts.

It was also in 1979 that I first heard about female circumcision, the cutting off of the clitoris, a practice which is still common in a number of Arab countries including Egypt. Circumcision is usually performed on girls when they are aged seven or eight. Traditionally, two women members of the family hold the child down while a third (or a midwife or doctor) cuts out the clitoris with a razor. I was horrified to hear of this form of mutilation, supposedly meant to preserve the virginity and chastity of girls by reducing their desire for sex.

The Egyptian writer and doctor Nawal El Saadawi has written that as a rural physician, she was often called upon to treat complications arising from this cruel operation. Infection and haemorrhage were common, and some girls died. The psychological shock of circumcision she found to be just as severe. Her research (1974) found that almost all 'uneducated' Egyptian families insist on circumcising their daughters, while two thirds of 'educated' families also retain this practice which they saw as a 'cleansing' or 'purifying' procedure.

To me, circumcision seemed a particularly horrible form of male domination and I am sure that Abdel-Salam saw a terrible storm brewing when he realized how much it appalled me. I told him to leave our flat and not to come back until he had found out whether it was a part of the Islamic religion. If it was, I said, I could not be a Muslim and I could not be his wife.

He soon returned and told me that female circumcision was not a part of Islam, and in this alone he was quite correct. He went on to reassure me that no daughter of ours would ever have to face it. He told me that fewer and fewer Egyptians were 'having their daughters done' as the word spread that this practice is not a requirement of Islam.

It is still hard for me to accept that he fooled me. Not only have I been told that circumcision of girls is now on the increase in Egypt, but I later found out that the women of his own family had been routinely circumcised. Ten years after our discussion in Cairo, he enabled his parents to take our daughter to a doctor in Cairo with the intention of having her circumcised. Only Yasmeen's determined resistance saved her from this dreadful ordeal.

By June, the heat had become almost unbearable. And when I thought it couldn't possibly become any hotter, it did. Opening windows didn't help: it was like turning a hot air blower on to yourself. I was taking cold showers about eight times a day in order to cool myself down. But even the water that came out of the cold tap was warm.

Now I understood why Egyptians keep their curtains and shutters closed. It is to keep out the relentless sun that drains everybody of energy. One night, I sat on the tile floor of our flat wearing a thin cotton nightie, trying to cool down but feeling as if my veins were about to burst from the heat. Finally, I rushed out on to the balcony in desperation, but as soon as I opened the balcony doors, I was covered from head to foot in voracious mosquitoes.

The heat was oppressive, my lifestyle was oppressive and my parents-in-law were oppressive. I was losing weight fast, as much through dehydration as through stress. I wondered if I would ever be the same again. Where was the light-hearted, happy-go-lucky girl I had once been? In Cairo I was becoming miserable and withdrawn, and yet there seemed to be no escape. Despite our endless visits to the Embassy, we seemed to be getting nowhere in our quest for a visa for Abdel-Salam, and I was beginning to despair of ever going home again. I had never imagined that one day I would wish that I was standing at Marble Arch in the pouring rain.

One day, I was feeling so desperate that I accused the entry clearance officer at the Embassy of being racially prejudiced against my husband. He was quick to point out that there was nothing to stop me from flying to Britain as a British citizen, but that the Embassy had the right to refuse entry to my husband without giving a reason.

I went up to the Consular Section of the Embassy and demanded to see the Consul, but while I was there a staff member hinted that the reason Abdel-Salam was having such difficulties in getting a visa was because we intended to settle in England. I left the Embassy that day knowing that I would have to lie to get my husband a visa. I hated the idea of lying, but how else was I to return to my country? The next time we visited the Visa Section I said that my sister was to be married and that I simply had to be there. I lied that we would return straight after the wedding. 'Come back next week,' we were told.

I was sick and tired of being told to come back next week – and I was also sick and tired of being in a foreign country. Egypt was no longer an adventure; it had become an ordeal. I wanted to be back in my own country where people understood what I had to say and where people shared my attitudes and assumptions. I could not be myself in Egypt, not just because of the language barrier but because of the cultural divide. Abdel-Salam's parents in particular still seemed to me to be like aliens from another planet.

We left the British Embassy exhausted, longing for the peace of our flat, but as we turned the corner of Rameses the Second Street, I saw people on our balcony. I was horrified: who could it be? Then I recognized my husband's brother Gamal on the balcony, surrounded by young men whom I had never met. They had obtained a key from the caretaker and as we came into the flat they shouted 'Surprise!' in Arabic. But I didn't want to be sociable with a crowd of total strangers who had entered my house uninvited and, calling Abdel-Salam into the bedroom, I told him that they would have to leave. I felt that my only refuge – the only place that I could be myself – in this strange country was my home, and now even that had been invaded.

Abdel-Salam tried to get rid of our unwanted visitors, but he was being too diplomatic to succeed. In the end it was I who opened the front door, said 'Goodbye', and made sure that they left. And then I went to bed, my head throbbing from the heat and from the stress of the visa interview.

I woke up angry, and with a lot to say. For four months I had been trying to get an entry visa for Abdel-Salam. I felt that, in the meantime, I had tried hard to fit in with Abdel-Salam's family and friends. I was learning Arabic. I had converted to Islam. But no matter what I did, it never seemed to be enough. I reflected on all the insults I had had to swallow from my father-in-law. I felt that I had been too soft in allowing Abdel-Salam's family and friends to think that they could change me.

I heard Abdel-Salam wake up, but I didn't rush to make his tea. Instead, I waited for him to come to me. And when he did, he brought tea for me and sat waiting for me to talk. I told him that I expected privacy in my own home, and that without privacy, I felt exposed and vulnerable. The message seemed to get through. Abdel-Salam apologized for his brother's behaviour and told me that he would tell Gamal to apologize to me. However, this conflict was minor compared to the extreme tension between my brother-in-law and me in years to come.

The next time we went to the British Embassy, I sat in silence in front of the Entry Clearance officer, having nothing new to say. Then, as I heard what he was saying to me and Abdel-Salam, my heart skipped a beat. He was telling us that he had decided to grant an entry visa to my husband, but that I had to write a letter stating that he would not be settling in the UK. I asked for pen and paper and wrote the letter immediately.

We were asked to wait outside, and I was still nervous: maybe this was a cruel joke? But when Abdel-Salam's name was called we were told to collect his passport from the cashier's window. Abdel-Salam had got his visa! It wasn't until we were out of the Embassy building that we threw our arms around each other, hugged and whooped with joy. 'Mabrouk!' (congratulations) said the soldier on sentry duty at the Embassy gates. I only knew that I would never take my country for granted ever again.

Abdel-Salam wanted to tell his parents our good news straight away, and so we went to Sharabiya. They knew from the looks on our faces that we had good news, and when I told them what it was, my father-in-law said, 'You are talking Arabic now – and yet you are leaving!'

My mother-in-law gave us the usual congratulations, and then she said to me: 'You are taking him away from me.' I asked her to visit us in London – in the unspoken hope that she would wait at least one year before a visit.

I couldn't wait to get home and introduce my husband to my family and friends. I had written to my sisters, telling them of my marriage and asking them to pass the news on to the rest of my family. (Queenie had written back to say, 'How romantic! Does he wear a turban?')

But now that we were free to go, I realized that I had mixed feelings about leaving Egypt. I felt that I was going home a much richer person. I had learned a great deal and I had met some fascinating people in Egypt. For the first time, I had lived in a country other than my own and Egypt had come to feel like a second home to me. Egypt was where I had come to know and love Abdel-Salam. It was where I had been married and set up home for the first time as a wife. Yet I was also eager to get back to England and to begin my married life there – without interference from Abdel-Salam's parents.

Before leaving for England, we went to Sukaria to say goodbye to the family. The family were all waiting for us – the uncles, their wives, children and Abdel-Salam's parents – and we all sat in a big circle on the grass in the shade of a tree.

Uncle Ibrahim's wife was breast-feeding her child. She looked so happy, feeding her baby so easily in such a natural setting. Abdel-Salam's mother asked me how much longer she would have to wait for a grandson. In my halting Arabic I told her that she might get a grand-daughter, but she would have none of it. 'We want a boy called Mohammed, like his grandfather,' she said.

I was feeling ill and tired and so I didn't argue with her; I asked Abdel-Salam if it would be rude of me to be excused to take a nap. One of his aunts led me into her bedroom, lent me a cotton gellabia and closed the door. I didn't care about the dirt and disarray; I wanted only the peace of an afternoon sleep.

The room was full of flies that kept buzzing and landing on my skin. I knew that I would never get them all out of the room, so I decided to cover myself completely with the cotton sheet. Still they were crawling on me – but how? I looked inside the bed thinking that some flies must have been trapped under the sheet. Instead I saw huge fleas crawling over my legs.

I screamed in horror, and jumping out of the bed, ran out of the house to where my husband was sitting on the grass, scratching my legs furiously as I ran. Oh for cool, rainy London. Oh to be stuck in a traffic jam at the Hangar Lane gyratory system. All in all, I couldn't wait to get back to England.

Chapter Eleven

We flew home on 26 June 1979. I savoured every second of that flight, anticipating all the things that I was going to do in England and all the places that I was going to see. More than anything else, I had missed being able to walk freely and easily in the streets. Now I wanted to parade around London with my husband, showing him off to everyone.

It seemed like only minutes before the Captain was telling us to prepare for landing. I gazed down at the Thames and felt that this beautiful green island was lifting my spirits and rinsing away the dust of Cairo. I had missed my country so much, and now it seemed that she was in full bloom and wearing a summer's dress to welcome me.

Just before landing, Abdel-Salam handed me his passport to 'take care of'. I began to explain that he would need it to get through immigration, but he cut me short, telling me that he had another passport for immigration control. I found out later that my husband was using two passports. One was his 'real', student's passport of only six months' duration – all that he was legally entitled to, having evaded his (compulsory) national service. The other had been obtained illegally by his father who worked as a driver for the Egyptian passport office: this was of longer duration and had been stamped with a visa by the British Embassy.

As we were about to land, I decided to leave the questions until later and put the passport in my pocket. Mohammed Taha greeted us warmly at Heathrow, and then there was the bliss of riding in a London taxi all the way to Bayswater. I relished the wonderful sights, sounds and smells of London. Punk rockers and scantily dressed girls reminded me of the freedoms I had missed in Cairo. We drove up Kensington High Street, past shops full of new fashions, and then we were pulling up outside number 8, Talbot Road, W2.

The room that Abdel-Salam had lived in previously was still available to us. It was far from luxurious and it would take hours to clean, but it was a start. And then, having caught up with our old friends in Mohammed Taha's rooms, we went for a walk under the green, swaying trees of Hyde Park. It was wonderful to see young couples holding hands and kissing in public after six months of having to sit on the chair furthest from my husband for propriety's sake. We drank cola at the café next to the Serpentine. I felt so light I was sure I could fly if I tried.

Mohammed turned to me and asked, 'What are those horrible spots on your face?' But nothing could spoil my reverie. 'They're freckles, Mohammed,' I told him, forgiving him because I assumed that darker skinned Egyptians don't get freckles.

Later that evening, Abdel-Salam and I, plus some of his friends, went out to Thursdays nightclub in Kensington High Street. It was where we had first met and it seemed right to go there on our return to London as man and wife. Mohammed was still working at Thursdays and had even arranged a job for Abdel-Salam in the same place. But my husband refused the work, saying that he didn't want to serve alcohol. (He did drink alcohol, but serving alcohol is considered by Muslims worse than drinking it.)

A few days after arriving in England, we took the train down to Brighton and had a happy, carefree day by the sea with our friends. Abdel-Salam remarked that day that as a

Muslim woman, I should have a Muslim name. He said the best name for me was Hebba t-Allah, meaning 'Gift from God', because I was God's gift to him. Soon afterwards I changed my name by deed poll to Hebba t-Allah Ahmed, and not until my children were abducted did I revert to using my original name.

Before long we made another train journey, this time from Victoria to Thornton Heath to visit my home town and the house where I was born. No member of my family, apart from Kath, had yet met Abdel-Salam. I loved walking with my husband in the streets where I had played as a child, and as we walked I found myself telling him everything about my childhood. I pointed out the street where I had learned to roller-skate and my first school. And then we were walking up to number 95 Livingstone Road, to the house where I was born.

I knocked on the door, expecting my father to open it. But it was my brother Christopher who opened the door. I said 'Hello, Chris! I'm back, and this is Abdel-Salam, my husband.' Christopher spat at Abdel-Salam and slammed the door shut in our faces.

I stood there in shock and embarrassment, not knowing what to say to my husband. My brother's behaviour was in painful contrast to the warm welcome I had received from my husband's family in Sukaria. My brother had a reputation for difficult behaviour, but why had he insulted my husband so unpleasantly? We went to the end of the street and from a phone box tried to telephone my father at his garage, but he wasn't there.

I then telephoned Queenie, who sounded happy to hear from me. But when I told her about Christopher's reaction, she said, 'Oh well, you know what Christopher's like. And everyone is against Abdel-Salam because Kath said that he called her a prostitute, and that you were treated like a servant in Egypt.'

I have since realized that Queenie and Christopher were racially prejudiced against Abdel-Salam from the start. It was true that in Cairo I had spent a lot of time cleaning and cooking for my husband, but no more than many other British wives. Abdel-Salam appeared to take it all with a pinch of salt, but I could see that he was really very offended. It would have been nice to have my family's blessing, but if we weren't going to get it, I decided, we would just have to manage without it.

I knew that my father would be more reasonable and when I did take Abdel-Salam to meet him at a later date, he was accepting and friendly. But I couldn't ask Abdel-Salam to visit my family again after the way that he was treated; Abdel-Salam never did see my family home and things remained very cool with my family, especially with Christopher. He did however see them on occasion, such as hospital visiting times when our children were born.

In the week before Christmas, Abdel-Salam began work at The Seashell, a famous and highly successful fish and chip restaurant and take-away in Lisson Grove, NW1. He was delighted with the novelty of working only five days a week with a whole day off in the middle of the week. It wasn't long before he became a favoured employee of the restaurant's owner, rising to the heights of deputy manager.

Meanwhile, I took a job as the manager of a small boutique in South Kensington. I was glad to be working and helping my husband to build our future, and every Saturday I handed over my wages to him proudly and with total trust. We were beginning our married life with a strong sense of optimism and I felt that we had everything to look forward to.

I was happily planning our first real Christmas together (we had missed out on the celebrations the year before in mostly Muslim Cairo) and I planned a traditional Christmas dinner with all the trimmings. We had invited all our Egyptian friends to join us, and I bought a tree complete with flickering lights. On Christmas Eve, Abdel-Salam and I sat in the semi-darkness together, drinking claret and watching the lights flick on and off.

Christmas felt very special indeed and something told me that it was not just because I had missed out on the year before. I had a tremendous feeling of well-being and I felt utterly content. I didn't know it then, but I was pregnant with my first child.

Abdel-Salam was delighted that I was pregnant and telephoned his family in Sukaria to tell them the good news and to ask them to pass it on to his parents (they didn't have a telephone in Sharabiya, although strangely, there was one in the village). I knew that I would have to stop working in the autumn of 1980 and – having left the boutique – I found temporary work at The Seashell alongside my husband. I hated it; my pregnancy was making me feel nauseous and the smell of frying oil made me feel even worse. I also felt that wrapping fish and chips was a comedown from my previous work, but I stuck at it as we needed the money more than ever before.

I finished working at The Seashell at the end of July and spent hazy summer days on the tiny balcony of our two rooms in Bayswater, dreaming of the child that was wriggling inside me. On the neighbouring balcony, a fragrant jasmine plant was growing and it brought back vivid memories of holidays in Tunisia and my first experience of Islam. I knew that if I gave birth to a son he would be named after my husband's father according to Egyptian tradition. But if my first child was a daughter, I decided, I would call her Yasmeen, the Arabic word for jasmine.

One day, after an ante-natal appointment, I called in to see Abdel-Salam at work to tell him that I had seen our child on an ultrasound scanner at the hospital. His education in Egypt had not prepared him for modern ante-natal care and he had never heard of ultrasound. He stared at me in disbelief. How could I have seen the baby, he asked. Did they take it out and put it back? He was desperately worried about his unborn child and the potential dangers of this new technology.

I went into labour on a Friday evening, the busiest time at the fish and chip shop, and Abdel-Salam turned up in his white overalls to drive me to hospital in the manager's Mustang sports car. He went back to work for a while and then came back to the hospital in time to see me being wheeled into the operating room for a Caesarian section. Abdel-Salam was terrified that he would be given the 'wrong' baby, and in the lift he heavily tipped the nurse to make sure that he got the 'Ahmed' variety.

I woke up in pain after the operation and asked for my baby. When she was put into my arms I stared in shock at the stranger I was holding. She looked almost Chinese with tiny pursed lips, a shock of fine black hair and long fingernails. But once she had begun to feed from my breasts, I wondered how I could ever have thought she was not mine; she was a tiny version of her father. My Princess Yasmeen had arrived.

Abdel-Salam had been given a week's holiday and he

arrived to visit us with an entourage of friends the next day. Some of my family arrived at the same time. When Abdel-Salam remarked in Arabic that he was glad my daughter didn't have an 'English nose' (i.e. a snub nose), my sister Kath asked for a translation and I stupidly provided it. She threw him a haughty look and – giving me a gift of a furry elephant for Yasmeen – said, 'This hasn't got an English nose either, I think it's probably Egyptian!'

I was also upset by remarks made by my husband's friends who said that Yasmeen looked completely Egyptian. It made me feel that I was no more than a factory for Abdel-Salam's baby.

Yasmeen and I were both poorly and in hospital for some time after her birth. I was recovering from the Caesarian operation, while Yasmeen was born with a congenital dislocated hip. After the agony of watching the doctors bend and twist her little legs, I was told that she would have to wear a splint. The splint made breast-feeding difficult as I couldn't cuddle her to me in the correct position and, before long, my breast-milk dried up.

Yasmeen screamed and screamed, while I carried her around, talking to her and singing to her. I was desperate for sleep, but the moment I dozed off, she would wake me with her screams. I watched the other mothers in the ward jealously as they bathed their babies, a task made impossible by Yasmeen's splint. Then the doctors, after taking X-rays, told me that Yasmeen would have to wear the splint for the first year of her life. I felt very worried and rushed to phone my husband: 'Yasmeen is ill and I don't like what they are saying.'

He arrived at the hospital after work and he was bursting with excitement. 'I'm going to take you and Yasmeen home in a Mercedes!' he blurted out, without a glance at

135

his daughter. I thought he had borrowed a Mercedes, but he had bought an eleven-year-old model for £1,100. That was more than half of our hard earned savings. I knew that a car of that age would be a liability and I was angry and disappointed. I also suspected that Abdel-Salam was jealous that I had found a 'new toy' in our first-born child, and that he had bought the Mercedes as compensation for himself.

It was wonderful to get home from the hospital. We had only two rooms, but they were safe, comfortable and they were ours. I proudly and carefully laid Yasmeen in the cot that I had prepared for her before my labour began ten days before. I tiptoed around our two rooms not wanting to disturb her much-needed sleep. Abdel-Salam prepared food that I felt too tired to eat, but I ate it anyway, to please him.

But that day was the first day of six intolerable months. Six months of Yasmeen screaming and of constant visits to the doctor. The tenants upstairs held nightly, noisy parties which left Yasmeen and me on a knife's edge of sleeplessness. Abdel-Salam however, spent most of his time downstairs in Mohammed's room, together with his Egyptian friends. It seemed that nothing in his background had prepared him for sharing the work of parenthood as I had hoped he would. As a result, Yasmeen became my sole responsibility from the very beginning.

One day, shortly after Yasmeen and I had arrived home, she cried and shrieked until I thought I would go mad with worry. I was sure that she was in pain from the splint and when I couldn't stand it any longer I went downstairs to fetch Abdel-Salam. I knocked on Mohammed's door and stood waiting. The music was loud and so I knocked again more loudly.

Immediately, the music stopped. The door opened slightly, and when Mohammed saw that it was me, he tried to close it again quickly. But I had caught a glimpse of the room and saw that a pornographic film was being shown there. Much to Abdel-Salam's embarrassment I insisted on going into the room and I told him that instead of watching sex films on his week's paternity leave, he should be helping me and his daughter in our flat.

He followed me meekly up to our rooms, past the party guests from upstairs falling over each other to get to our shared toilet. Yasmeen was crying hysterically. Abdel-Salam looked at her and had no idea of what to do. It was swiftly becoming clear to me that the care and protection of my child was a job that I was going to have to do alone, and without the active support of my husband.

Chapter Twelve

For six long months, Yasmeen wore the splint that divided us in so many ways, denying us both proper hugs and cuddles. On our latest visit to the hospital the doctors had told me that the splint should be left on until her first birthday when they would decide whether or not corrective surgery was necessary.

My daughter seemed to be the focus of attention for most of the trainee doctors at the hospital and I was beginning to doubt their diagnosis. As I pushed her pram through the streets of London, my little Princess sobbed in great gulps and sucked her thumb. I knew it was the examination that had upset her, and vowed that I wouldn't let her go through that ordeal again. Halfway home she was still sobbing wretchedly and I took her out of her pram for a cuddle, whispering in her ear, 'Last time Yasmeen, we're not going there again.' I had resolved that we would get private medical treatment for our daughter, and I had also decided to trust my instinct to take off her splint when we got home.

I stopped at a chemist and bought baby bubble bath and a yellow plastic duck, and when we got home I prepared a bath for her in front of the fire. It was the first time that I had bathed my baby since she had been born and I lowered her very carefully into the lovely warm bubbles. At first she threw up her arms in surprise, but it wasn't long before she was kicking her legs in a frenzy of excitement and giggling happily. I was soaked, but I didn't care: we were thoroughly enjoying ourselves and I didn't want her first bath to end.

When I lifted her lovely, slippery body out of the water to wrap her in a warm towel, she wriggled and laughed and we cuddled up close next to the fire. No splint! And she smelled wonderful and felt warm and cuddly. This was one of the moments I had been waiting for throughout my pregnancy and that afternoon Yasmeen and I made up for all the cuddles we had missed since her birth.

Within a week Abdel-Salam and I had taken Yasmeen to see a private doctor who specialized in orthopaedics. After giving her an X-ray, he told us that Yasmeen didn't need to wear the splint – and that she probably never had needed it. We drove home much relieved, with Yasmeen kicking and cooing in her carry-cot, and I felt that I could begin to enjoy being a mother for the first time since her birth.

But unfortunately, there had been a distinct change in Abdel-Salam's behaviour towards me since our daughter was born. He had become very critical of the way that I dressed. One day I had driven down to see Queenie in Croydon with the sun roof open and Yasmeen gurgling with joy on the seat behind. I felt that I had finally settled down after the birth, and that at last, everything was going well.

When I got home, I was wearing a pair of jeans that my sister had given me, and although they were still two sizes larger than my pre-pregnancy size, they still made me feel young and free. Abdel-Salam was waiting on the balcony, and I hurried upstairs to greet him, but he did not seem pleased to see me. He was coughing nervously in the way that meant he had something difficult to say and eventually he managed to spit it out: 'You are a mother,' he said. 'Don't wear jeans any more, they are not respectable.'

Just as I was beginning to feel like myself again, Abdel-Salam had deflated my high spirits. It was the first of many times that he would hurt my feelings and undermine my achievements. Another occasion which illustrated the differences in our backgrounds was my birthday in March of 1981. This was my first birthday as a mother and I craved special attention from my husband on that day. Abdel-Salam told me that birthdays were very rarely celebrated in Egypt. In his village, birthdays were considered much the same as any other day of the year and his mother didn't even know her own date of birth.

However, as the birthday cards arrived in the post from my family, Abdel-Salam realized that he was amiss in ignoring my birthday. When we went out to the shops to buy his Egyptian newspaper he picked up a card and asked me, 'Will this one do?'

'You're not supposed to show it to me,' I hissed. But bless him; how was he supposed to know that? His upbringing was so different from my own that he had no way of knowing that he was supposed to buy me a card – at the very least – on my birthday, and to keep it a secret. Abdel-Salam was the closest person to me of all, and yet he was a world away from me – despite his apparent integration into London life.

Yet it was a lovely birthday card, covered in roses and written with love, and it took pride of place on top of the TV at home.

In March of 1981 we moved into a new flat at 41 Lisson Grove. It was only three doors away from The Seashell where Abdel-Salam was working, and it took up the first and second floors above 'Ken's Junk Shop'.

I was especially pleased that our landlord – who was the owner of The Seashell – had, at my suggestion, converted the flat roof into a patio, and I planned to grow many pots of flowers in the sunshine. Abdel-Salam was doing very well in his job and his boss continued to be very good to us.

It was spring, the time of daffodils, blossoms and new beginnings, and we had our own front door and a bathroom of our own. Yasmeen lay cooing and aahing on the soft velvety carpet and everything smelled of new paint. That night when Abdel-Salam came home from work, I was feeding Yasmeen before putting her back in her cot for the night. 'Oh, what a cosy sight, honey!' he said to me, and he was right. Despite the cultural differences between us, our marriage was for the most part good and secure. Although in the long term those differences did prove too much for us – Abdel-Salam's expectations of marriage were not mine – at the time we enjoyed a wonderful feeling of promise for the future.

All too soon it was time to get packed for our month's holiday in Cairo. We had promised Abdel-Salam's parents that we would bring their new grandchild to Egypt, and I was looking forward to returning to Cairo as a mother. I was also relieved to know that – with money sent by Abdel-Salam – my parents-in-law had moved from their two squalid rooms into a better apartment. I was quite happy that my husband had sent money to Cairo to help his parents. I had learned that in Egypt, the average person is very poor indeed and has little to support him or her in life apart from religious faith. We had sent money periodically so that Abdel-Salam's parents could escape the worst of their poverty, calculating that they needed a deposit of some £5,000 (sterling) to lease a flat in a good area.

To my disappointment, we had sent no more than £400 when we heard that my parents-in-law had rented a new flat in the same run down district of Sharabiya as their previous flat. Abdel-Salam explained that his mother had not wanted to move out of the community for fear of losing contact with her long-time friends and neighbours. His mother could not change the pattern of a lifetime by moving to a 'posh' area, he said.

And so the move took place to number 5 Hussein Mahmoud Street, El-Sharabiya. I was upset at the time to think that it was rather a miserable move. Nine years later, when my children were abducted to that same address, I discovered that it was an even more miserable move than I had first supposed.

In December 1982 it was my parents-in-laws' turn to visit us in London. I was expecting my second baby, and remembering the difficulties I had faced at the time of Yasmeen's birth, I wanted Abdel-Salam's parents to be with us when the new baby was born. At least, I thought, they would be able to help with Yasmeen if I had another Caesarian birth. But in my need for support, I was turning to the wrong people.

My parents-in-law had been in England for no more than two weeks when I went into labour with Sawy, but already I was desperate to escape the oppressive atmosphere at home. My mother-in-law and I had very different views on child-rearing and it was her idea of spoiling their grandchild to let her run riot. Yasmeen had started to refuse her food and to stay awake through the night. I felt that my authority as a mother had been undermined and that I wouldn't get it back until the grandparents had gone home to Egypt.

In the event, I was happy to escape to the hospital where Sawy was born quite naturally on Christmas Eve at 6.25 p.m. He looked like a little lion when he was born, with streaks of ginger in his hair. From the start, there was perfect understanding between Sawy and me. I knew from the second that I first held him in my arms that he would never be any trouble to me, ever. He was a heavenly baby, breast-feeding like a dream and sleeping soundly for hours at a stretch. Even when he cried it didn't jangle my nerves: I just picked him up with confidence and fed him. I had a son as well as a daughter! I felt very powerful and accomplished.

As soon as my mother-in-law arrived at the hospital to see their grandson she ordered me, 'Give him your breast!', as if I was going to starve him. I told her, 'I've just finished feeding him Mama!', but she said, 'Give him the other one then!' Yet there was nothing which could disturb the happiness and closeness of Sawy and me.

Yasmeen came with her grandparents to meet her new brother. I was all too aware that she might feel jealous, and so I had bought a life-size baby doll for her as a present on this occasion. When she came into the ward I said to her, 'Come and see your baby brother – and here is his Christmas present to you.' Yasmeen kissed her brother's head and said thank you to him, naming her dolly Amira, which means princess in Arabic.

As for my baby's name, this was predetermined by the death of Abdel-Salam's younger brother, who had recently died after having a fit. His parents insisted that my baby must be called El-Sawy in his memory.

I asked the hospital to circumcise Sawy in the days after his birth, in keeping with Muslim traditions. I believed that this minor operation would be less traumatic for him in the first days of his life. However the hospital said they would not circumcise Sawy as it was not medically necessary.

Sawy was finally circumcised six weeks later, at home, by a 'doctor' whom Abdel-Salam had met at the Regent's Park Mosque. Yasmeen still remembers the day that her brother was circumcised on the dining table, although she was only two years old at the time. She says she will never forget how Sawy screamed and cried and then went suddenly, frighteningly, quiet.

Male circumcision should only take about five minutes, but Sawy's ordeal lasted forty-five minutes. I was told to wait outside the living room while the operation was taking place, but when I realized that it was all taking too long, I became afraid for my son and went into the room. I rushed to the table and saw that my baby was extremely pale: Sawy had gone into shock and was not making a sound. The 'doctor's' hands were shaking. Abdel-Salam said I shouldn't look: at that moment the 'doctor' was pulling back the foreskin very hard and cutting the bit underneath.

I knew then that this 'doctor' didn't know what he was doing: in circumcision the foreskin should be pulled forward over the penis, and then after a quick snip, the operation is over. This 'doctor' was literally breaking Sawy's foreskin off. Blood had soaked through his nightie and through two layers of towelling on the table. His foreskin was left on the dining table next to him.

My heart was hammering out of fear for Sawy and I carried him away from the table and held him in my arms. He could not cry, but he was making strange gulping noises. I put him to my breast to feed and comfort him, but for the first time in his life, he refused my breast – and he never fed from my breasts again.

It wasn't until after the circumcision that I discovered that the man who performed this barbaric act was not a qualified doctor, but a Cairo medical student who had come to London to study. I was extremely angry with Abdel-Salam about all this – Yasmeen too was very disturbed – and I never forgave my husband for putting his son through such a trauma.

Chapter Thirteen

In the summer of 1983, Abdel-Salam's parents phoned to tell him that his brother Gamal had become engaged to a young girl in Sharabiya. Gamal had failed to get good enough marks at high school to qualify for college, and had been called up for National Service. However, his father had bribed officials so that Gamal spent his National Service lounging around the house and getting under his mother's feet. Small wonder that she agreed to the engagement.

But Abdel-Salam wasn't happy. He argued that his brother was too young to think of settling down and that he didn't have the means to begin married life. Abdel-Salam all but ordered his brother to come to England for a visit, and employed a lawyer to apply for Gamal's visa through the Home Office in the UK. It was a tactic that probably made the immigration officials suspicious, and Gamal was informed that the visa section were not satisfied that he wanted no more than to visit the UK.

Abdel-Salam became very depressed, arriving home from work late at night to sit with his head in his hands, desperate for his brother to come to England. I couldn't stand another moment of it. If getting Gamal a visa would dispel the dark cloud over our household, then I would get him his visa.

I flew to Cairo in January 1984 with Yasmeen (aged three) and Sawy (aged one). I was also six months pregnant with Sammie. It had been a year since I had seen my parents-in-law and I wondered how we would get along this time. I wasn't looking forward to the visit. I knew that I would have to fight off the panicky feelings of being trapped that Abdel-Salam's parents induced in me. But I hoped that things might be different now that I had produced two grandchildren and had another on the way.

At Cairo airport, Yasmeen ran towards her grandmother and Sawy was whisked from my arms by his grandfather. I had my arms empty of children and, suddenly, I felt lost without them. When we arrived in the flat in Sharabiya we were very tired and I wanted to bath the children and put them to bed. But their grandparents had other plans and insisted on playing with the children until the small hours. I was annoyed that my parents-in-law seemed to take over my role so easily. It was as though I had lost my authority over my children and they were encouraged to do things that I had forbidden them to do at home. I knew that my children would have to relearn a different kind of behaviour when we got back to England – and that it would be very hard work for me.

I had brought tinned food for the children, but the grandparents insisted that we all eat the same food. So the children ate with us and within twenty-four hours they both had gastroenteritis.

I did give the children a bath on that first night, but it was a dismal and frightening experience. The grandmother sealed us all into the flat, locking every window, and encouraged Yasmeen to help her carry saucepans full of boiling water to fill the tub. (There was a water heater in the flat, but it hung uselessly on the wall, no more than a status symbol.)

My mother-in-law was still a world away from me, and I had long since decided against trying to reach her. Instead I chose to accept her as she was, hoping that she would return the compliment.

The oppressive atmosphere in the flat strengthened my resolve to get Gamal's visa as quickly as possible, and we went together to the British Embassy on 3 January. I told the Entry Clearance Officer at the Visa Section that I had travelled to Cairo specifically to sponsor my brother-in-law for a visa to the UK for a holiday. I told him that in my condition, I didn't want to have to return to Cairo again. The next day Gamal and I heard that his application had been successful and we collected his passport with the prized British visa stamped in it. Together we went to the nearby Semiramis Hotel to phone Abdel-Salam in London with the good news. He was absolutely delighted.

His mother was not so pleased. She said to me resentfully, 'You took Abdel-Salam away and now you're going to take Gamal too!' His father, however, was glad to see his son go: 'What's he going to do here?' he said. 'He's lazy and good for nothing and he carries bad luck with him wherever he goes.'

A seed of suspicion was planted in my mind: was Gamal planning to live in England? But I remembered that Abdel-Salam had told me he wanted his brother to holiday in England, hoping that it would broaden his outlook and end his plans to marry. Later that evening I asked Gamal about his plans: he told me that he loved his country very much and had no plans to settle in England – although he might stay for longer than one month. I had met his fiancée Nihad, and it certainly seemed that the young couple were serious. And after all, Gamal was unlikely to get the chance to holiday in England after getting married.

We had another week to wait until the formalities were completed and Gamal could fly with us to the UK, and so I planned an outing to the Pyramids with the children and their grandparents. To me, it was almost a pilgrimage: my marriage had begun right next to the Pyramids and I wanted photographs of my children with these ancient tombs as a backdrop.

My parents-in-law had spent their entire lives working like Trojans and they had very little idea of how to enjoy a day's outing. We drove up Pyramids Street and then up the winding road which leads to the foot of the Pyramids – and then the grandfather stopped the car, lifted Sawy up in his arms and exclaimed, 'Yanhar! El-Haram!' ('Look! The Pyramids!'). He then expected us to go back home to Sharabiya. It took a lot of persuasion from me to get him to park the car and let us walk around for a while: weren't his grandchildren half Egyptian, and didn't he want them to soak up a bit of Egyptian history? When I suggested having a coffee as well, he was astounded. 'We've got coffee at home,' he said.

I spent the rest of the week in Cairo watching my children crawling around the floor of their grandparents' home in Sharabiya. I couldn't relax my vigilance for a moment because my parents-in-law had such different ideas about children's safety. One day I took Sawy to the sink to clean his bottom. His grandfather came over and pulled Sawy's tiny soft legs apart brutally, and of course the child screamed blue murder. The last thing a child with gastroenteritis wants is to have such rough treatment.

I hid in the bedroom with my children for the rest of that day and night, longing to go home. At intervals the grandparents would bang on the locked door and Yasmeen would shout, 'Git out, git out!' They mistakenly thought she was shouting, 'Giddou, Giddou!' (grandfather, grandfather!) and so they knocked all the more.

I found some relief in talking to Gamal who was at least closer to my age than my parents-in-law. He confided in me that his father didn't love him, and that he couldn't wait to get away from him because they didn't see eye to eye.

We flew home at last to England on 10 January and Gamal was very nervous indeed. It was his first flight and he refused to take off his heavy mackintosh and sat sweating and staring around him as if he were demented. I knew that as soon as we were airborne he would deluge me with questions about what to say to the immigration officer at Heathrow, and I was right.

We flew over my beloved Pyramids and I relished the sight of the sun glinting on them. I reflected on how much I had to look forward to: I had a new baby on the way and I knew that my husband would be so proud of me for bringing his brother to him.

I felt sorry for Gamal during that flight. He was so unworldly and so afraid. He flatly refused to look out of the window, and two hours into the flight he was still wearing his mackintosh. He wanted to go to the toilet but I could tell that he was afraid to get up and walk down the aisle. I got up and went to the toilet myself, hoping that it would help him to overcome his fear. The plug in the bathroom sink was missing however, and I was concerned that the alarming noise it made when water drained away would upset Gamal further.

Gamal did find the courage to go to the toilet and I watched to make sure that he was OK. He emerged in a terrible state. His flies were still undone and he was trying to do them up as he walked. I knew that the sink had terrified him, but I didn't say anything about it for fear of offending him.

We arrived at Heathrow with Gamal still in his mackintosh, and sweating all the more for terror of the immigration officer. He didn't allow himself to relax until we were collecting our baggage and walking through customs to meet Abdel-Salam.

'Alf Humdillah Salam!' I said to Gamal as we walked out into the arrivals hall: 'One thousand welcomes.' Little did I realize that Gamal was bringing with him all that I had found most oppressive about Egypt – and that his influence on my husband was to spell the beginning of the end of our marriage.

It was a joy to see Abdel-Salam so happy. His smile stretched from ear to ear as he and Gamal hugged and hugged. It brought tears to my eyes and reminded me of when my sister Kath had arrived in Cairo almost five years earlier. Abdel-Salam hugged and kissed me too and told me that he had missed me very much indeed.

We drove home – the brothers talking all the way – and unpacked the Egyptian food that their mother had sent over for Abdel-Salam. I wandered around my home happily, enjoying its luxury and comfort, and felt very glad to be back. I turned on the hot water tap just to feel the lovely hot water, and then I gave the children a bubble bath. My husband came upstairs and held me tight, saying, 'Thank you Bunny, I love you so much.' It was as if I had pulled off a small miracle.

All freshly bathed, I changed the children into their best clothes and we set off to show Gamal our latest venture.

Abdel-Salam had recently left The Seashell Restaurant, and borrowing money from various sources, had gone into partnership with a man called Emad Gaffer. Between them they had set up their own restaurant, The Seashore, with Abdel-Salam as the manager.

I walked proudly into the restaurant, arm in arm with my husband and my brother-in-law. The staff fussed over us all, carrying the children about and welcoming Gamal. I was free to look around, and after the squalor of Sharabiya, the sparkling clean smoked-glass tables, the gleaming chrome chairs, the candles and rosebuds on every table seemed like a dream come true. I reflected on how lucky Abdel-Salam and I had been, and on how much we had achieved since our return to London five years before. I was the Guvnor's wife, and I was loving every minute of it.

The next day, life returned to normal. I drove Yasmeen to her private nursery school in St John's Wood and then drove home again to cook for the restaurant. Every day I baked six apple pies, made fresh taramasalata and tsatsiki and laundered the staff uniforms. Then I drove to the restaurant to deliver them. Everywhere that I went, my little Sawy came with me, cooing and gurgling in his car seat. But far from feeling overworked, I loved every minute of it, feeling that I was helping my husband to build a future for us all.

Gamal was soon bored at home and spent more and more time at the restaurant with his brother. It wasn't long before Gamal began working (illegally) at The Seashore. I was relieved that Gamal was no longer in the flat all day – I had begun to feel like his entertainments manager – but I still didn't suspect that Gamal's presence would influence Abdel-Salam to behave more and more according to traditional Egyptian values.

In February 1984 the brothers both went down with flu, and they lay about the house moaning and groaning and sneezing their germs all over the children. I sped around the house, nursing the men and constantly collecting and disposing of used tissues that they left on the floor for me to pick up. One day I found Sawy sucking on a used tissue, and I became very angry: 'For God's sake,' I bellowed at them, 'can't you think of the children?'

And of course, the children did catch the flu – a particularly virulent strain – and so did I. After weeks of being nursed by me, Abdel-Salam and Gamal had recovered, but now that I was ill they expected me to manage on my own. I could hardly breathe and suffered pain in my lungs. Sawy and Yasmeen were hardly sleeping and needed constant attention. But when I spoke to my husband he said, 'You'll be all right, you've only got a cold, not the same flu that I had!'

I was eight months pregnant, caring for two small children and the baby I was carrying had not kicked for days. I became so ill, tired and depressed that I insisted Abdel-Salam come home and call the doctor. After the doctor had diagnosed a severe chest infection and had given me antibiotics, I asked him to have a quiet word with my husband downstairs, to impress upon him that I needed help with the children.

When the doctor had gone, Abdel-Salam came upstairs and said: 'Why did you tell the doctor that I don't help you? I have given you a beautiful home and two beautiful children. You had nothing until you met me. I dragged you out of the gutter and gave you a home. Not even your family care about you; they never come to see you.'

I felt terribly upset: if the flu didn't finish me off, my husband's hateful words would. Besides, his words weren't true. I was in regular contact with my sisters, but – partly because of the tensions with Abdel-Salam – I would take the children to visit my family, rather than vice versa. Was Abdel-Salam still ill, I wondered? Why was he talking to me like this?

One night, I heard Abdel-Salam's voice in the kitchen, and desperately in need of company and comfort, I went downstairs to sit with my husband and brother-in-law. As I went into the living room they both looked up as though I were intruding on their conversation, and the room fell silent. I offered to make tea for us all and as we sat together I felt more and more that they were talking to each other because they had things to say that they didn't want me to hear.

I wondered if perhaps my illness was making me feel paranoid, and I went back to bed.

Gamal had been living with us for almost two months and there was no sign that he might leave. By now I very much resented the way that his presence had changed my life. Abdel-Salam's attitude to me and the children had changed a great deal since his brother's arrival.

Gone were the cosy chats that I once waited up for when Abdel came home from work late at night. I no longer waited up: I went to sleep rather than face another rejection. It was as if he no longer needed me and he treated his family as if we were a liability.

One night I overheard my husband and Gamal discussing how they planned to go out to nightclubs in order to find a British bride for Gamal. Abdel-Salam was advising Gamal on how to snare a woman, and how to exploit her nationality. 'They're only good for one thing,' he told

Gamal. 'They're all shit and they deserve to be used. You have to treat them like shit; if you're good to them they don't appreciate it.'

I couldn't believe that my husband really meant what he was saying, and I wondered if he was going through some kind of mental crisis. He had been working very hard, often waking before dawn to buy fish at the fish market, and then working until midnight. Or perhaps he was just showing off to his brother? Perhaps he thought that this behaviour was masculine in some way? Whatever the reason, I would have to do something if I was going to save our marriage.

The next night I bathed and perfumed myself and waited for my husband to return from work. My plan was to tell Gamal that I needed to spend some time alone with my husband: I knew that he would be embarrassed and would leave the room.

It worked, and Gamal excused himself and went to bed. I made tea for Abdel-Salam and sat down with him at the table as he worked out the day's takings from the restaurant. When I found the right moment I said, 'Abdel-Salam, we have to talk. Since your brother has been here you have changed. You are always sharp with me and I feel that you don't love me any more. I don't feel wanted. Perhaps it is because I'm pregnant, and maybe I'm being oversensitive, but I just want to know that you still love me, darling.'

He turned to me, his features hard and cold, and said, 'Look, you have to know from now on that I can lose you but I cannot lose my brother.' His words hit me as hard as any slap. I wondered if I had misunderstood. I almost wished that he would tell me some lies to reassure me. I just needed comfort and to feel wanted.

'You do still love me, Abdou, don't you?' I asked him.

His voice was icy: 'You are shit. You have always been shit. We have an expression in Egypt that says, "If a dog's tail is curved, you can straighten it, but it will always curl again."'

I stared at him as though I was seeing him for the first time. I couldn't speak. I just stared at him in shock, feeling numb and confused as a strong sense of hatred began to overtake me. Our third child was still in my womb and I was feeling hatred for his father. I vowed to myself that this child would be all mine and nothing to do with Abdel-Salam. I could not think of him as the father.

Abdel-Salam left the room without another word and went straight upstairs to sleep. I heard him say goodnight to his brother, and the next sound I heard was his snores.

That night in March 1984 I divorced Abdel-Salam from my mind and my heart. I cried hard and long, and the sadness that I felt was so very deep and profound that I felt as though my tears were of blood and that my life was draining out of me.

I remembered how, five years before, Abdel-Salam had told me that we were married in the eyes of God because we had made a commitment to each other. But now, we were no longer married in the eyes of God; only a certificate bound us together.

I was deeply concerned for the baby inside me. I worried that my sadness would damage him in some way, seeping into him so that he would feel sad even in the safety of my womb. But the next day, I decided that my sadness would not be allowed to affect my children's lives. If I put on a brave face and a smile, I reasoned, then surely I would be happy eventually.

I thought too about the practicalities of bringing up three children alone, and about the distress that they would suffer if I did legally divorce their father. I decided that I should try to make a go of my marriage, if only for the children. I told myself that the children's needs must take priority.

Yasmeen was three and a half; Sawy was fifteen months. I would keep very busy and enjoy those special years with my children, in spite of the secret that I held inside me. I was worried about Sawy, however. His speech was slow to develop and he expressed himself in grunts and shouts. I felt sure that he was angry and wanted more attention and I decided that – with the new baby due in a few weeks' time – the restaurant would have to do without me.

And so I became even more separate from Abdel-Salam. He stayed in the role of breadwinner, while I saw to his needs when he came home. And he couldn't fault me in my role of supermum and housewife. Leaving myself no time to think, I made sure that my home was always spotless, and that my children were well dressed and well cared for.

Every Sunday I entertained Egyptian friends of Abdel-Salam's who came in droves for the food that I prepared. Looking back, I see that I was desperately covering up for the failure of my marriage, but for the time being, I could not see what else to do.

Gamal had only been in England for one month before he found an unwitting young girl to provide him with all that he dreamed of: a resident's permit that would lead on to permission to work and British nationality. I listened with gritted teeth as I overheard Gamal and Abdel-Salam discussing tactics.

Gamal had met Sophie in the same nightclub that Abdel-Salam had met me. I began to wonder if Thursdays shouldn't have a warning notice pinned to its walls: 'This is a haunt for foreign nationals looking for extensions to their visas.'

Sophie came from a respectable Sussex family and she seemed to be a naïve and thoroughly confused young girl. She told me proudly of how she had met Gamal at the bar of Thursdays and of how she had made the first approach. Sophie was working as a secretary while sharing a flat in London with girlfriends. She had only known Gamal for two weeks when he proposed, and I could hardly believe that she had accepted so quickly. Gamal proudly told his brother that Sophie wanted an intimate relationship with him, but he had told her that sex was out of the question because he was a staunch Muslim.

Sophie came to see me and asked me how I had met Abdel-Salam. She wanted to know all about our marriage, and she asked me why Gamal wanted to get married so quickly and did I think he was genuine? I told her that she must make up her own mind on that subject and that it was not for me – as her would-be husband's sister-in-law – to advise her. Without telling her directly that she should have nothing to do with Gamal, I tried to indicate to her that she should think again. 'If there was anything wrong,' I said, 'I could not tell you, or my husband would find out and he would be furious.'

Yet Sophie seemed determined to marry Gamal and the date was set for March 1984. I refused to attend the wedding because I couldn't bring myself to witness a marriage that I knew was not genuine in intention. I felt guilty enough about aiding Gamal to enter the UK, and I couldn't bear to watch another British girl being used for visa purposes in the way that I felt I had been exploited.

And Gamal's new status after his marriage (he was now

an official British resident and on his way to being a citizen) gave him untold confidence. He displayed this by freely insulting me in front of my husband, who stood by without coming to my defence. Gamal began to be excessively strict with my children too.

One day, in the restaurant, Yasmeen was dancing to music and Gamal slapped her for what he considered to be bad behaviour. I was furious and told him never to touch my children again. He told me, 'I am just like their father; I am their uncle and they must do what I tell them.' From that day on I did not bother to disguise my deep dislike for Gamal.

My dislike was fuelled even further as I heard him talking to Abdel-Salam about his plans for the future. He intended to marry again in Egypt once he had been granted his British nationality, telling his brother that this was his right as a Muslim. If Sophie didn't like it, he said, she would just have to put up with it. Already he was treating Sophie like dirt.

Then one day in 1984 there was a programme on television about female circumcision. I recorded it to show Abdel-Salam. He had told me that female circumcision was rarely practised in Egypt any more, and yet some of this film had been shot in Cairo. As we watched it, Gamal arrived and I was horrified to hear his opinions on the mutilation of young girls.

'What is the problem?' he asked. 'Why are you so upset about this?' He told us that not only is female circumcision still practised in Egypt, but that all of his female cousins in Sukaria had been 'cut'. To give Abdel-Salam credit, he did try to explain to Gamal that female circumcision is not a requirement of Islam, and he tentatively spoke about how it denies women pleasure in sex. Gamal's response was that sex is not important for women because women are only for producing children.

All-out war was declared between Gamal and me that day. I threw him out of the house and warned my husband that if he were to defend his brother, he could follow him out of the door. I pointed out that we were living in England, where women have strong rights under the law.

It was as if the three-cornered conflict that had happened in Cairo between Abdel-Salam and Kath (with me caught between them) was repeating itself on English soil. Only this time, I was the spouse defending the values of my country while the two siblings were Abdel-Salam and Gamal. The difference was that in Cairo, I had tried to keep both my sister and my husband happy – whereas Abdel-Salam now joined his brother in an alliance against me.

When Gamal had gone Abdel-Salam told me, 'If we were in Egypt, I could divorce you for what you have just done and I could throw you out on the streets without even your clothing.' I doubted it very much; I knew more than he thought about women's rights in Egypt. But I was shaking with anger. Since Gamal's arrival, my marriage and my children had suffered. I wished fervently that I had never volunteered to go to Egypt to get Gamal's visa.

Chapter Fourteen

On 23 March 1984, my beautiful sunny Sammie was born, just as England was covered in bright yellow daffodils and spring sunshine. It seemed to me that the earth was celebrating my son's arrival. Yasmeen and Sawy came to visit their new baby brother at the hospital, and I was amazed at the difference in size between Sammie and Sawy. I had thought of Sawy as the baby until now, but when he came bouncing into the hospital ward he seemed huge in comparison to his new brother.

Sawy had a look at the baby, and then he looked up at me, sucking his thumb, and with his eyes he said, 'So what?' Then he ran off to play, totally ignoring me and the new addition to the family. But I knew that Sawy was putting on an act: it was going to be hard for him to adjust to the fact that Sammie was going to take up his mother's time, drawing attention away from him.

Sammie's birth had been easy compared to the births of his two siblings, and with his arrival I again felt that strange sense of identity and power which my children brought to me. I felt there was no mountain I couldn't scale; no problem I couldn't solve. I was now the mother of a beautiful, intelligent daughter and two gorgeous sons. My motherhood filled me with a complete sense of accomplishment. And Sammie was a dream of a baby. He breast-fed easily and then he slept for four hours at a time – which was just as well really, with two other children to care for.

The children and I had become a unit, quite separate

from Abdel-Salam. I often marvelled at how we managed to live together, but I knew that many married couples lived for years in just the same way. I would smile rather cynically to myself while people complimented Abdel-Salam and me on our successful marriage and our happy family. If only they knew.

I had lost faith in my marriage and in the notion of marriage in general. I had decided that so-called happy marriages probably didn't exist, and I decided to count my blessings and make the best of what I had. And my chief blessings were three children who were a constant and surprising delight and who filled me with intense joy and pride.

Yasmeen was a real beauty with her grandmother's radiant complexion and her father's dazzling green eyes. Her hair was a luxurious mass of silky waves and curls, and she would sit patiently as I carefully blow-dried her hair into different styles. I would stare at my Princess as she slept, and dream of her future.

Sawy was so very special. From the time of his birth we had communicated without words. Even at fifteen months old I knew that Sawy was sensitive, creative and a dreamer. He was also fiercely loyal to his mum. He would sit, sucking his thumb dreamily, with his head slightly to one side, and his clear blue eyes would fix on mine lovingly. Through his beautiful eyes he would express himself with such clarity that words were not necessary.

Every now and then he would say quietly, 'Mama', and I knew that he was telling me that he loved me. His looks were half mine and half his father's: I could see my mother and my brother in his face, and yet at the same time, his Minofian ancestry melted through his features.

And Sammie was all me, blond and tiny and skinny. He looked so English that the waitresses at The Seashore would ask Abdel-Salam, 'How is little Lord English today?' – which annoyed him intensely.

Yet as much as I enjoyed my children and my motherhood, it was testing to live with and to sleep with a man who had no regard or respect for me. Sex with Abdel-Salam had become a serious problem. It was no longer the gift that it once was; it had become a duty that I was expected to perform, a part of my role as a wife. It certainly wasn't making love any more, and even when I wanted to let go and relax, I denied myself. Yet I always felt as though I had been a traitor to myself after we had had sex. But if I refused my husband, he would sulk like a child and his mood would disturb the balance of our home and ultimately, our children.

The tension inevitably showed itself in my life and was a drain on my health and mental well-being. My GP had given me tamezepam (a mild tranquillizer prescribed to treat depression), but still I found myself worrying unduly about things. Abdel-Salam later claimed that I was 'crazy'. After Sammie's birth I had had my tubes tied, which Abdel-Salam had agreed to at the time. (I'd even checked with his mother that this was not against Islam.) He later claimed that this was against the will of God and – in the tradition of men who believe that women are ruled by 'hormones' – he ascribed all my unhappiness to the want of another baby.

I would spend hours on the phone to my sisters who told me time and again that I was worrying about things that were beyond my control, and that this was a symptom of depression. They told me that I would be better off without Abdel-Salam and that caring for my children on my own could not be worse than the tension of living with him.

But I would hear none of it: at that time I was still telling myself that it was better for my children to have both their parents together. The truth was that I put up with my marriage for three years longer than I wanted to because I thought it would be easier for myself and my children than going through a divorce.

Things were also going downhill fast at The Seashore Restaurant. For the first six months, things had gone very well and the restaurant had been taking some £3,000 a week. But then, for some reason, trade stopped very abruptly. Emad Gaffer, who was not involved in the day-to-day running of the restaurant, needed to report to his sisters in Cairo (they had invested their inheritance of £15,000) on the progress of the business.

Abdel-Salam's accounts were vague and he resented being questioned about the business. Before long he was under suspicion of mismanagement. Emad brought in an independent consultant to supervise the management of the restaurant, while his sisters arrived from Cairo to investigate. Abdel-Salam reacted angrily to the criticisms, and the relationship between the partners degenerated swiftly. One day there was a terrible fist fight in the restaurant between Abdel-Salam and Emad, with Gamal aiding his brother. Emad was badly beaten and was admitted to hospital where he nearly lost his left ear as a result of the violence. Still Emad tried to make peace with Abdel-Salam, but to no avail.

I found myself in a dilemma as to where my loyalty lay. Emad had secretly told me of his despair at Abdel-Salam's attitude, and Emad's wife Rose had become a close friend of mine. I knew that Abdel-Salam was not keeping his business partner well enough informed and I too had my suspicions that he was mismanaging the restaurant. Yet he was my husband and the father of my children and I had supported him in this venture.

Emad then brought in an independent accountant who

scoured the books for errors and eventually asked Abdel-Salam where the profits had gone. I watched as Abdel-Salam stood up and slapped his pockets, a clear indication that all the profits had gone to him. It was more than Emad could bear. A few days later he changed the locks on the restaurant and he and his family staged a sit-in.

Abdel-Salam saw his dreams going down the drain. He had grown tired of being a 'worker': he wanted to follow in the footsteps of other Egyptians who had arrived in England almost penniless yet had made their fortunes here. He talked constantly of the Egyptian owner of Harrods, but his talk was full of jealousy. Abdel-Salam wanted to make a quick buck, and he had begun to think of himself as some kind of tycoon.

As a result he had borrowed money (including £5,000 from his own father and £4,000 from an Egyptian friend) to go into partnership with Emad. He had given up a good job of deputy manager at The Seashell – where he had many perks including a rent-free home – to make his own way in business. Yet now he had upset Emad and he was in danger of losing everything.

Abdel-Salam's response was to pay £1,000 to a lawyer in order to take out an injunction against Emad. I was forced to stand by helplessly, knowing that anything I said or did would be seen as disloyalty for which my husband would punish me with extreme verbal abuse. Meanwhile my friendship with Emad's wife Rose had been destroyed by Abdel-Salam's insufferable behaviour.

On top of all that, our landlord, the owner of The Seashell Restaurant where we had both worked previously, was now taking legal action to evict us from our home. I felt that the security, respect and promise that we had not so long ago enjoyed was disappearing fast.

At home too, Abdel-Salam's behaviour became more and more dictatorial and I began to call him 'Hitler'. One day, Sawy hung on to his knee, pleading with his dad to open a can of drink for him. I watched incredulously as Abdel-Salam exploded with rage and ripped off the top of the can, then hurled it across the room.

Sawy immediately put his thumb in his mouth and came to me sobbing 'Mama'. Abdel was behaving as if his children were no more than a nuisance which I should attend to, while he dealt with 'high finance'. And despite the long hours that I put in helping with the restaurant, it was as if his wife and family had become nothing more than a financial and emotional burden.

In 1985, Emad Gaffer died of a heart attack behind the fishpans at The Seashore Restaurant. I was devastated by the news, but his wife Rose's mental health was destroyed. In the same year, having been evicted from our flat by our former boss, we were made homeless. The Council put us on the eleventh floor of a tower block off Edgware Road in central London, where we survived for nearly a year before moving to a council house in Maida Vale.

The children were stuck in the middle of this unpleasant situation, and they clearly suffered from all the strife and insecurity. In the summer months of 1987 I would often find Yasmeen crying quietly in her bedroom. She wrote notes and left them where I would find them, saying, 'I wish I were dead', and 'I wish I were one of the stars I can see from my window; stars are cold and dead.'

This was my precious Princess for whom I had such high hopes. At the age of eight she asked a health visitor at the child health clinic, 'What is a prastute?' – because she had so often heard her father insulting me and calling me a prostitute. I had always been an entirely faithful wife, yet

Abdel-Salam often used this term to express his deep-seated misogyny. On my initiative, Yasmeen began seeing a child psychotherapist to help her cope with her distress.

Sawy too was having nightmares and waking up racked with sobs. One night I sat with him, stroking his hand to help him wake gently from such a nightmare while he cried out in his sleep 'No, no, don't hit me!' It was obvious that the children were suffering from our continuing partnership.

In 1986 I went to the Regent's Park Mosque with Abdel-Salam and a Muslim mediator to seek guidance and advice from Sheik Khalifa, a religious counsellor. The Sheik listened to my side of the story and then he questioned my husband. Everything that we said was said in front of each other and in front of two independent Muslim witnesses. I was hoping to be granted a divorce under Islamic law.

After I had put my case – that my husband had abused me verbally and emotionally, branding me a prostitute in front of my children – Sheik Khalifa turned to my husband, told him that he had been wrong in his behaviour towards me and warned him that divorce was my right under Islamic law. But then he asked me to give Abdel-Salam another chance by staying with him as his wife for another two weeks, and then returning to him for marriage guidance counselling.

As soon as we had left the Mosque, Abdel-Salam said to me, 'That is absolutely the last time that you talk to anyone about any problems between you and me. You are my wife and you must do as I tell you.' I didn't see the point in going back to the Mosque: things had gone too far to be salvaged in this way.

My attempts to discuss the situation with Abdel-Salam had come to nothing. He seemed to think – as he had been brought up to think – that women simply put up with their husbands. As far as he was concerned, he was getting his meals, sex when he wanted it and the children cared for – so what was the problem? As his wife, he believed, I belonged to him and divorce was unthinkable.

In April 1987 I went to see a solicitor to ask for advice about divorce, and in July – after Abdel-Salam's behaviour became even more dictatorial and aggressive – I began divorce proceedings on the grounds of unreasonable behaviour. I had hoped for an amicable arrangement, but I knew that Abdel-Salam saw divorce as the ultimate rejection, and that it was not going to be easy.

My first priority was the physical safety of my children and me. The day that I began legal proceedings, I called a locksmith to change the lock on the doors of our house in Maida Vale, arranged for the children to be cared for elsewhere – and telephoned Abdel-Salam. When I told him what I had done, he slammed the phone down and I knew that he was on his way home in the car. I paid the locksmith and ran to a friend's house for sanctuary.

The children and I spent the next few months creeping in and out of our home trying to avoid a confrontation with an angry Abdel-Salam. When we did see him, he would sometimes be aggressive – and sometimes conciliatory. I never knew whether I was going to get a punch on the nose or a bouquet of roses.

In January 1988, I was awarded custody of the children, and in March our divorce was made final. I had custody, care and control of the children and Abdel-Salam had open access. However, within six months, my ex-husband had upset and disturbed the children so seriously that I went back to my lawyer to take action to deny him access.

Yasmeen had begun to act as if she was afraid of me. I

discovered that he had told Yasmeen that I had married very young and had had a baby – and that I had murdered my baby and my husband. I immediately told Yasmeen that I had married young, and told her that George had remarried and was living happily not far away. The 'baby' was a figment of Abdel-Salam's imagination.

He also told my sons that 'all English women are rubbish': a disturbing thing to say to children with an English mother and a father who married an Englishwoman. He also instructed the children to make a stand against me by refusing to go to school. He told them they should tell their teachers that they would not do any more school work until mummy agreed to be daddy's wife again.

On 17 April 1989, Abdel-Salam's birthday, I collected the children from the Bayswater school and took them to a newsagent's shop to buy a card for their Dad. As we walked towards home, I noticed his car parked outside the house of an Egyptian friend and we went into the house to give the card to him.

To begin with, Abdel-Salam seemed glad to see us; but before long he had started shouting at me and insulting me in front of the children. Suddenly, he stood up and punched me, making me fall back against the mantelpiece. When I fell to the floor, he started kicking me. There was uproar. The children were screaming and trying to pull him off me, while his Egyptian friend stood by, doing nothing.

I shouted at the children to run into the street and wait for me. God knows how I managed it, but I ran out after them, my face covered in blood, and hailed a passing taxi. We went straight to Harrow Road Police Station where I reported the incident and asked for police protection for the children and me.

After that, we walked in fear that Abdel-Salam would be

lurking somewhere on our Maida Vale estate, waiting to attack me again. I decided that we would have to move away from the area. We needed a clean break and a fresh start for the children. Abdel-Salam's lawyer negotiated with mine and we settled for an amicable agreement with 'defined access' – on the basis that my ex-husband would restrain his violence and would stop saying disturbing things to the children. We agreed that he would see the children between four p.m. and eight p.m. on Thursdays and between ten a.m. and eight p.m. on Sundays.

Then in April 1989 he married again. His bride was a twenty-one-year-old from Egypt called Effet Shadid. Abdel-Salam had been working for a year in a Kilburn supermarket owned by Effet's brother, Sarwat Shadid, and it was here that they had met.

Abdel-Salam boasted to me that she was a virgin, and certainly she was naïve, immature and lacking in confidence. She was jealous and apparently frightened of me, and until she got used to me, she used to shake with nervousness whenever we met.

It seemed however, that his marriage was having a good effect on Abdel-Salam, and after a few months his behaviour towards us improved. In retrospect I know that he was beginning his campaign of softening me up in preparation for stealing the children, but I had no way of knowing that at the time. Before long, I allowed Abdel-Salam open access again.

And this marriage to Effet was destined to end unhappily, just as mine had. In the flat in Cairo, Yasmeen later told me, Effet used to confide in her that she was going to divorce Abdel-Salam as soon as he came back from the 'Red Sea' (he was in fact in America) to marry her childhood sweetheart.

Effet did leave Abdel-Salam, taking divorce proceedings within two days of my being stabbed by the grandfather. She was terrified of what Abdel-Salam would do to her after her charge Yasmeen had been taken away, and it is very likely that – having seen my blood-soaked body on the floor of the El-Salam Hotel – she wanted to avoid the same fate.

Chapter Fifteen

In 1989 Abdel-Salam moved to Cricklewood with his new wife, whereas I decided to move to Mitcham to make a fresh start and to be near my father. Although this was a time of great sadness – my father died in hospital only two days after we arrived in Mitcham – it was also a time of new beginnings, and it seemed as if Abdel-Salam had changed very much for the better.

I encouraged the children to respect Effet and to be friendly with her, and Abdel-Salam was behaving very nicely to me and the children. He took us for days out at the seaside; he would drop in to see us, bringing bags of much-needed groceries; he invited us to Cricklewood for Sunday lunches cooked by Effet. In retrospect it is clear that he was trying to lull me into a false sense of security before abducting the children.

On one occasion I had even raised the subject of children being stolen from one parent by the other. He said, 'I would never take the children from you. You know as well as I do that the mother is the most important person to her children.'

Yasmeen, who loved her father (and still loves him), pleaded with me to be allowed to stay temporarily with Abdel-Salam and Effet in Cricklewood. Although I came to regret it deeply, I agreed to let her go, while Sammie and Sawy stayed with me in Mitcham. And while Yasmeen was in Cricklewood, Abdel-Salam worked on her to persuade me that we should all go on a holiday to Egypt that September.

I was reluctant at first, but with Yasmeen pleading to be allowed to visit her grandparents and Abdel-Salam behaving in such an apparently generous fashion, my resistance was eventually worn down.

Abdel-Salam was offering to pay for us all to fly to Cairo. I had just begun a course in fashion design at Croydon College, so I could not spend four weeks in Egypt, but Abdel-Salam said he would buy me a ticket to join him and the children for two weeks of their four-week holiday. It seemed unfair to deny the children this opportunity, and after the death of my father, I was also feeling that a few weeks of sunshine would do me good.

I agreed to the idea – on the condition that the children would not have to stay for more than a few days at their grandparents' run down flat in Sharabiya, which is no place for a holiday. Abdel-Salam also promised he would take the children to Alexandria for a week. It never crossed my mind that he would never bring them back to me.

On 24 September 1989 I drove up to Cricklewood with Sammie and Sawy to collect Abdel-Salam and Yasmeen to take them to Heathrow. I noticed when we were saying goodbye to Effet that she was giggling uncontrollably. I said to Abdel-Salam, 'What's up with Effet?', but he said, 'Oh, take no notice.' (I was told she would join them later in the month, but in fact she flew to Cairo later that day.)

We sat together in the café at Heathrow, the children in their best clothes, Sammie and Sawy playing with boomerang planes that I had bought for them. The only indication from Abdel-Salam that he was at all nervous came when we walked to the departures gate and he asked me to stay at the airport for a while longer 'in case there is any trouble with immigration'.

I dismissed the idea: how could there be any trouble for a

father taking his children on holiday? But Abdel-Salam knew in his own mind that what he was about to do was wrong, and he must have had a paranoid sense that the immigration officials would discover his plan. I kissed the children goodbye, telling them I would be following them on another plane a week later, and went home to Mitcham to do my homework.

I phoned them in Cairo at ten o'clock that night, but Abdel-Salam said they were too tired to talk to me; he was putting them to bed and I agreed to ring back the next day.

The next day I went to College and walked home, enjoying the lovely autumn sunshine. I put a ready-cooked meal in the oven, enjoying the luxury of not having to cook for the children, and rang Cairo again. Immediately, hearing Abdel-Salam's nervous coughing, I knew that something was wrong.

He said, 'I've got very bad news for you. You are never going to see your children again. Don't talk, just listen. If you ever want to see your children you have to agree to be my second wife. You have to come to live in Cairo. You must give me your passport and you must come into my home with your shoes in your mouth.' (This is an Egyptian saying for accepting humiliation.)

I said, 'Don't do this to the children', and pleaded with him to be reasonable. He wouldn't listen and I hung up as if the phone itself had given me a shock. Then I phoned my sisters who were both supportive and urged me to ring him back to try to persuade him to change his mind. But nothing I could say to Abdel-Salam made any difference. He said, 'My children are with me and my wife is with me' – as if I had been replaced and my motherhood stripped away. When I said that I wouldn't agree to being his second wife, he put the phone down.

I called the police in Mitcham to say I wanted a warrant for Abdel-Salam's arrest. I knew that he wouldn't stay in Egypt for long – there was no way that he could earn enough in Cairo to support Effet and the children – but I was told that as the children had left the country with my permission, there was little that the police could do.

I phoned the British Embassy in Cairo and spoke to the Consul. In my naïvety about child abduction, I believed that the Embassy would assist me, and I asked the Consul if he would help me fly the children home if I could get them to the Embassy.

I was upset and disappointed to be told that because the children were dual nationals (it was then that I learned that my children were dual nationals and that they were also Egyptian nationals), the Embassy could do little for me. The Consul's concern was to avoid a diplomatic incident. I felt very much on my own.

I phoned the lawyer who had arranged my divorce and made an appointment for the next morning to get a court order for the return of the children. (I eventually got a court order, but soon discovered that, in Egypt, it was not worth the paper it was written on.)

I also rang Sarwat Shadid, the supermarket owner who was Abdel-Salam's boss and Effet's brother. I asked him: 'Do you know that your sister has helped Abdel-Salam to kidnap my children?' Sarwat said that he didn't know, but that Abdel-Salam had been talking about abducting them for the past three months.

Why hadn't he told me, I demanded? Because, he claimed, he couldn't find my new address. I told him that I could not accept this excuse, and he promised to put me in touch with a good lawyer in Cairo.

*

Why had Abdel-Salam taken the children? I still don't fully understand his motives. It certainly wasn't because he wanted to be with them, or why would he abandon them to the care of Effet and his parents so soon after arriving in Cairo? I suspect that he felt that I was still his wife under Islamic law, and he may have believed that I would be blackmailed into accepting his demands that I should live as his second wife. Perhaps he was also avenging himself on me for divorcing him by attacking me where I was most vulnerable – through my children.

I can't begin to describe my feelings of desolation and loss at what had happened. On my own in the house in Mitcham that night, I blamèd myself again and again for letting the children go. If only I hadn't believed Abdel-Salam; if only I hadn't been selfishly tempted by the idea of a trip to Egypt; if only I had said no . . .

I remembered the times when, tired or exasperated, I had said to my children, 'Go away and leave me alone.' And now I was alone, and now they had gone.

Chapter Sixteen

I had to raise money quickly to get to Cairo and to pay for lawyers. I sold my car for £275. My brother David gave me £500. My sister Kath gave me £1,000. An Egyptian friend of the family gave me £500. I flew to Cairo on 12 October 1989.

From London, Sarwat Shadid had arranged for me to consult a prominent Egyptian lawyer, Sayeed Al-Mahmoudy, when I got to Cairo. At the airport I was met by two junior lawyers from the office of Sayeed Al-Mahmoudy. One of them was Medhat Al-Zohiry, who was to do most of the work on my case for the next two years. They took me into Al-Mahmoudy's offices in central Cairo where – although it was late at night – many offices were still open, making use of the cool evening hours after closing in the heat of the day.

I felt very nerve-racked. On top of the grief and stress of the cruel separation from my children, I was in a strange environment and dealing with strangers in a foreign language. Everything that was happening was beyond my previous experience and I had no way of knowing whom I could trust. Yet I had to get it right: to fail to win my children back was unthinkable.

I spent an hour and a half in conference with Sayeed Al-Mahmoudy, whom I distrusted on sight. He was smarmy and all smiles to me, but he was a bully to his staff, constantly interrupting our conversation to shout at them for more coffee or for different files.

Al-Mahmoudy wanted some £5,000 (sterling) for taking on my case, and I handed over an advance payment of £1,500 (sterling). He had been recommended to me by an apparently helpful Egyptian in London, and I had no one else I could ask about lawyers' fees in Cairo. It was only later that I discovered how shamelessly he had exploited my desperation.

I gave Al-Mahmoudy a letter from Abdel-Salam's bank manager which asked why he had used his credit card to buy goods to the value of £1,700 when he didn't have the funds to cover that amount. Clearly, Abdel-Salam had been on a shopping spree knowing that he was leaving the UK.

I also gave Sayeed letters from the children's schools stating that they were expected back in school in London by 24 October, and that they had only travelled to Egypt for a holiday. I also produced a court order from the British High Court ordering my children's return, plus my divorce certificate. Each of these documents had been translated into Arabic at my expense before I flew to Cairo.

Sayeed Al-Mahmoudy said that he would make two petitions to the Egyptian courts. The first would be a straightforward custody petition. The other would be a 'short cut' to custody proceedings by getting my British court order for custody recognized under Egyptian law. Sayeed also told me that in Egypt, boys under ten and girls under twelve automatically belong with their mother, as long as she has not remarried.

It was one a.m. when I finally left Sayeed Al-Mahmoudy's office, to be driven to the outskirts of Cairo where I was to stay with Zeinab Abdel-Menaam – an old family friend of Sarwat Shadid's – and her husband. Zeinab, a journalist on the leading Egyptian magazine *October*, welcomed me warmly and for the duration of my stay, showed me the greatest kindness and hospitality.

Every morning for the next three weeks I travelled into Cairo with Zeinab in a women-only compartment of the Metro. There, I would visit my lawyers' office between hopeless forays into the Cairo streets to search for my children. At last I heard that my court hearing was set for 7 November, but Sayeed Al-Mahmoudy assured me that it would be adjourned, and I was scheduled to fly home to the UK on 3 November.

I wasn't going to leave without seeing my children, but Abdel-Salam defied a Public Prosecutor's Order – even after two days in custody – and refused to bring them to his solicitor's office to see me. Finally, hours before my flight from Cairo airport, I was able to meet them in the Public Prosecutor's office. They were anxious, upset and fearful of expressing themselves in front of their father.

I had seen their drawn, unhappy faces. I had seen their need for their mother. I was never going to abandon them.

It wasn't going to be as easy as I had first hoped to get my children back. I was in for a long haul; six months I thought, or perhaps even a year. The best way for me to proceed was to get as much publicity for my story as possible.

Once I was back in Mitcham I sat down and had a quiet word with myself. What did I have going for me in my fight to win my children back? I spoke Arabic: since Sammie's birth, I had been going to evening classes and had become quite fluent. I was also a Muslim: that would count in my favour in Egypt. And I had spent the years before I got married working as a demonstrator at exhibitions, which meant that I had considerable experience in selling and promoting. I would use those skills now to sell my story and to promote my cause, raising money to get myself to Cairo for the custody battle.

One of the first things I did was to make a poster of pink card, saying, 'Save My Children' and explaining my story. It had precious photographs of Sammie, Sawy and Yasmeen stuck to it. I worked very hard, taking the poster around the local pubs, asking pub managers if I could hold raffles.

I also rang virtually every national newspaper with my story, but to begin with the *Daily Mail* was the only paper to take any interest. They published a story about the 'Love Tug Mum' in November. The next call came from the *Croydon Advertiser* who sent their journalist Jackie McKeown. She wrote a story headed 'Love Tug Mum Has to Raise £5,000'.

After that, my telephone started to ring with offers of money and support. It was a great comfort to me to know that people cared and that the media were paying attention to my children's plight. By a stroke of good fortune, the drama *Stolen*, which told the story of an abducted child, was on the television at the time, and my case was taken up by various newspapers as a real-life example of this situation. My aim was to earn enough money to go out to Egypt again in January for the next court hearing (there had been two further adjournments since November). I was so busy that I barely noticed Christmas, although Christmas Eve, Sawy's birthday, was a terrible day. I went back to one pub where I had held a raffle the night before to reclaim my pink poster with the children's photographs: the landlady had thrown it away.

The day before I was due to fly to Cairo in January, the *Evening Standard* rang me to suggest that their reporter

Caroline Davies fly with me to Egypt to report on my case. The *Standard* had no money to give me, but they did help with the expenses of the trip, and Caroline's presence was a tremendous support to me.

In court I heard that my case had been adjourned yet again. It was a bitter disappointment, but I was determined to stay in Cairo until I had seen my children. My lawyer was refusing to negotiate with my ex-husband's lawyer, but while we waited for other arrangements to be made, I took Caroline to meet Sarwat Shadid's parents at their Cairo home. Sarwat's father claimed to have worked in the Presidential office and showed us pictures of himself with Nasser, Sadat and President Carter at Camp David. It seemed likely that he was a man of the world with some influence, and before long he had told me that he could help me. He said he was sure that he could arrange for my children to be rescued – but that it would be expensive.

In an extended string-pulling exercise, Caroline and I were introduced to a series of high officials who in turn introduced us to a politician who said he would help us to see my children. This politician sent emissaries to Abdel-Salam's parents, demanding that they bring the children to the National Party headquarters in Sharabiya. When the grandfather replied that the children were in Sukaria, the politician sent for the grandfather.

A horrible atmosphere of hatred and venom entered the room with him, and the politician told him that he must bring the children; that it was against Islam to keep them from me – and that it was bad for Egypt. The grandfather, not wishing to offend a politician with influence, agreed to bring the children in the morning.

The next day, 12 January, Caroline and I bought presents for the children (I had been unable to give them anything for Christmas or for Sawy's birthday) including a large chocolate gateau from the Nile Hilton. As we waited in the National Party headquarters, the grandfather arrived and told us 'my son refuses to allow his children to see their mother'. The politician became very angry and insisted that the children be brought to the office that very day. For my part, I lost my temper, hurling the gateau at the grandfather: it missed and hit the wall.

Caroline and I went back to our hotel, showered, had a brandy and bought another gateau. When we went back to the politician's office, it was jammed with people. Sensing that my children were about to arrive, I looked out of the window and saw my children in the back of a red Peugeot on the other side of the road. They were trying to get out of the car, and Abdel-Salam was preventing them.

Someone went down to negotiate with him, while I – knowing that the National Party would hate an unpleasant drama on its doorstep – leaned out of the window and wailed in my most theatrical voice, 'I am only a mother; I only want to see my children!'

Abdel-Salam sent a message that I could come down to see the children for two minutes. I said no, and he was persuaded to bring the children up to see me. They came in with their heads bowed, looking really frightened. Yasmeen sat nervously on the edge of the sofa. I said to the children, 'You tell me your news first, and then I'll tell you mine.'

Yasmeen began what was clearly a rehearsed speech: 'Well, mummy,' she said, 'I want you to know that we are very happy here in Egypt and we don't want to come back with you to England.'

I said, 'That's rubbish, Yasmeen, you can speak the truth to me,' at which poor Yasmeen looked at her father and then looked back at me, her eyes clearly telling me that no, she couldn't speak the truth in present company – without bringing punishment down upon herself. Abdel-Salam's response was to begin insulting me. In Arabic he shouted that I was a prostitute and a drug addict.

There was uproar in the room as voices rose higher and higher. My children sat whimpering like puppies on the sofa: Abdel-Salam had driven them from the village without cardigans and they were cold and miserable. Then, after no more than three minutes in my company, Abdel-Salam said that it was time for the children to leave.

I couldn't help myself: I picked up a tin of chocolate teddies biscuits which I had bought for the children and hit him on the head with it. Caroline was saying, 'Stop it, Pam, stop it, you're screwing everything up,' but I had been provoked too much. Then the children were gone and I was left to my distress.

The whole dreadful scene had been witnessed by a government official from the offices where the grandfather worked, and this man told the grandfather that he must take me in his taxi and follow Abdel-Salam and the children to Sharabiya. The grandfather at first refused, but when the official said, 'You don't want to be posted to Luxor, do you?' he changed his mind.

Grandfather refused to allow Caroline to come with us and I set off with grandfather in the official's car, arriving outside the Sharabiya flat only moments after Abdel-Salam drew up there with the children. Realizing that I was in a notoriously dangerous slum area with my worst enemies, I was afraid, but I went over to the car to see the children.

Abdel-Salam wouldn't let them out and tried to drive away, but one of the politician's security guards (Caroline had dubbed him 'Bruiser') stood in the path of the car to prevent him leaving. Abdel-Salam then got out of the car and tried to hit me, and with the children watching from the car, I passed out on the pavement.

Someone must have carried me up the stairs, because I woke up on the sofa with three little heads looking down on me. 'Drink some Pepsi, Mum,' said Yasmeen, but thinking someone might have poisoned it, I thought I had better not. Sawy came and sat with me. The room was full of people; neighbours, family members and security men assembled for the next scene of this drama. Someone said to me, 'I don't blame your husband for taking the children; they are so beautiful.' As if they were toys. I thought – my God, I am in the midst of enemies.

I stayed with the children for about an hour and a half while they told me about school and their day-to-day lives. I wanted to speak to them privately to tell them that I had not abandoned them but that I loved them and wanted them to come home with me, but this was impossible. Yet when it was time to leave I did manage to say quietly, 'Don't trust your father; he tricked us all. I didn't mean you to live here.'

I went back to the National Party headquarters to collect Caroline (she had been taken to the police station where, to her relief, she found the police merely wanted to offer her hospitality) and from there to the Nile Hilton.

Having only been allowed to see the children under the most stressful circumstances, I flew back to London to begin another round of publicity and fundraising.

As one court adjournment followed another in Cairo throughout 1990, it was clear to me that the only way I was going to get my children back was to rescue them myself.

Madiha Luxour, the prominent Egyptian custody lawyer who works on my case, told a BBC *First Sight* (1991) documentary that there are not enough judges in Egypt to hear custody cases. When asked what parents of abducted children can do about this situation she said, 'I advise them to snatch their children away (without my intervention). This is not a crime.'

Back in London I campaigned hard, keeping my case in the public eye, holding more raffles and sending out begging letters. I wrote to celebrities, to politicians, to the Queen, the Prince of Wales, the Princess of Wales, the Prime Minister and the Foreign Secretary – among others. I was buoyed up particularly by the sympathetic and supportive response I received from ordinary people who wrote to me after television appearances and newspaper reports, often including sums of money for my fighting fund.

Early in 1990, Sarwat Shadid's parents telephoned from Cairo to let me know that they had contacted a team of men who would rescue my children. This was going to be costly they said; the team expected to be paid £3,500 (sterling). In February I flew back to Cairo accompanied by Sarwat Shadid and his daughter (apparently there was no one who could take care of her in London). I was asked to pay for all of the tickets, which cost some £350 each. Shadid insisted I stay at the Sheraton Hotel in Cairo for five days after our arrival at the cost of around £500 – to prevent my path from crossing that of Abdel-Salam or one of his friends. After that, I was allowed to move in with Sarwat's parents, but I was not allowed to leave the house in case I was seen. I handed over £3,500 to pay for the 'team'.

One night I disguised myself in headscarves and was taken

to meet this team. I was introduced to a man in Egyptian military uniform who claimed to be a colonel. He said he could lead a gang of soldiers in a rescue attempt. But first he questioned me: was I Muslim? Was I able to care for my children in the UK? He needed to ease his own conscience. But the rescue attempt never took place. Later, at his parents' house, Sarwat Shadid said to me: 'We have been talking to high up people and we can't do the job because there is a file on you an inch thick in every police station in Egypt.' At the time I thought this was nonsense, but other people have since told me that it was very probable that all my activities in Egypt had been watched. I told Sarwat I wanted my money back, and he handed me an envelope containing only £1,000 (sterling). Sarwat Shadid had had a holiday, taken his daughter to Egypt – and been paid £2,500 for his pains. For my part, I had been ripped off again.

I flew home to London and more campaigning, returning to Cairo in March. I rented a flat and decided that I would base myself in Egypt until I got my children back. I hoped that being a resident of Cairo would improve my chances in court. I also tried to get a work permit and to get a job – which would prove to a judge that I could support the children – but I was denied a work permit because I wasn't Egyptian.

Early in 1990 Yasmeen wrote me a note on a scrap of paper which, with extraordinary bravery, she secretly carried with her for two days before picking someone she trusted (Effet's sister, Azza) to deliver it. The note read:

Dear Mummy,

I want to see you. Come, come, come, come to me. Phone me. Anything. I love you whatever happens, wherever I live.

Love from Yasmeen

186

She signed it with a picture of herself, crying. It broke my heart to read it. How could I explain to her that I was not being allowed to see her?

On 21 March 1990 (Mother's Day in Egypt) I managed to track the children down to their school in Shoubra, Cairo. It was a visit I had arranged myself (I simply called at the school), and I was frightened by Yasmeen's response to me. When she saw me she screamed, 'No, no, you want to take me away', and ran away. She was terrified that she would be punished for seeing me. Yet she had already written me a note pleading to see me – and had been punished by her father for it.

The note which she had smuggled to me had been published in the London *Evening Standard*. Yasmeen's Uncle Gamal had sent a copy of the paper from London to her father in Cairo and he had responded by locking her in her room without food for ten days. She survived this trauma with the help of her little brothers who managed to keep pieces of bread and tomatoes to give to Yasmeen at night. No wonder Yasmeen was terrified of the consequences of meeting me.

Yasmeen later described the visit to a journalist:

I knew Daddy had warned Mummy that if she ever came to Egypt he would kill her and bury her so no one would ever find her, so I was very scared about her being there at all.

On Mother's Day, Mummy managed to get into the school (her third visit after one at the lawyer's office and one at the Sharabiya flat). Again she brought us presents, but when the teachers brought me to see her, I suddenly felt really confused. I started screaming my head off. I think it was because Daddy had said she would change my name if I lived with her, and also because he had threatened to beat me if I saw or spoke to her.

Mummy looked upset and asked why I was crying. So I told her. Then she kissed me and I felt better. She gave me a present and I introduced her to my schoolfriends.

Every time I saw Mummy after that I wrote her letters and sent them to her hotel. Because my letters were in English I told my grandparents they were to ask her to stop the court proceedings, but really they all said: 'Come and get me as soon as possible.'

I never received these letters. Yasmeen had no idea where I stayed in Cairo. Who took her written pleas for help to me and tricked her into believing that I would receive them?

In between my attempts to see the children, I carried on going to court almost every month. But each time I received either an adjournment or bad news. On 17 April 1990 I lost the case to have my UK divorce and custody documents recognized in Egypt. This was devastating news, and although Helen Holmes tried to break it to me gently, I fell apart. The judge had ruled that my UK court orders could not be recognized because custody comes under Islamic law in Egypt and so bears no relation to the laws of England, a predominantly Christian country. It was time to think again.

The next eight months were a constant round of court appearances in which I tried to get custody under Egyptian law, flights back to London to raise more money, and attempts to rescue my children. From the time of the children's abduction in September 1989 until December 1990, I had raised some £15,000 to fight my case. I had travelled to Cairo over a dozen times and I had sat through over twenty court adjournments. In London I had sold most of my personal possessions, and the house in

Mitcham was now without television, telephone and much furniture.

After the visit to the school I managed another four visits to my children, going into Sharabiya by myself and knocking on the door of the grandparents' flat. Each time I was watched over very carefully by the children's grandparents who had ordered the children not to speak to me in English, not to sit next to me and not to say that they loved me.

I also saw the children many times without them being aware of my presence. Disguising myself with headscarves, I would go to the children's school playground and follow them home from school. I wanted to see how they were, but above all I wanted to know every detail of their daily routine, so that when the time came I could rescue them. On several occasions I got on to the bus with them after school. Once I even sat beside them, but I could not reveal myself: they must not know of my plans to rescue them in case they let it slip to the grandparents. Once, I saw Sammie fall over in the street, cut his knee and begin to cry: it was all I could do to stop myself from running up to comfort him.

In May, my lawyer Medhat and I met the taxi driver Mohammed who put us in touch with one team of men after another who claimed they could rescue my children – for a price. In the summer of 1990, the 'Brigadier' and his men botched the attempt to rescue the children from the grandparents' flat in Gezr El-Suez. In October, 'The Fridge' and his team ran terrified from the school playground, leaving my children behind locked gates as I sat, distraught, in a nearby car.

In December I went to the flat in Sharabiya to find a desperate Yasmeen. Only days beforehand her grandparents had attempted to have her circumcised. She was understandably terrified that they would try again, and she begged me to save her as soon as possible.

On 11 December I managed to rescue Yasmeen, but Sammie and Sawy ran away in different directions. I was cornered by the grandfather who stabbed me repeatedly, coming very close to his aim of murder.

Part Three

Chapter Seventeen

In November 1991, one year after I had survived a knife attack by my former father-in-law on the streets of Cairo, I returned to Egypt to give evidence at his trial for attempted murder. I was not only seeking justice for myself; I was hoping that the trial might put pressure on my ex-husband's family to release Sawy and Sammie back into my care.

Once in Cairo, I went to the office of my lawyer Miss Madeh Ahmed, who was deputizing for Dr Nabil Helmy (he had offered to take on my case after reading accounts of the stabbing in *El-Akhbar*). Madeh took me step by step through the procedures of the criminal court so that I could be quite clear about what would happen on the day of the trial. Madeh suggested that I also go to the same court – as a member of the public – to watch a criminal case in the days before the grandfather's trial.

I wanted to be certain about what tactics the defence lawyers might take – and what accusations they might throw at me. I had read the Chief Public Prosecutor's statement, containing the evidence of my two little boys, and I knew that they had been forced by their grandparents to lie about me and about the knife attack. I know that my children love me, each in his own special way, and I hated to think what lengths their grandparents had gone to in order to make them 'give evidence' against me. Yasmeen had already told me of the horrifying mental and physical abuse that she and her brothers had suffered at the hands of that family, and I was well aware that threats and violence would have been used to extract these statements from my sons.

And it was obvious – in several parts of the document – that my children had been told what to say. Sammie had told the Public Prosecutor that there were five men involved in the snatch attempt and that they all carried knives. (There were in fact four men, and none of them was armed in any way.) He also said the incident took place at 'six fifteen a.m.' Since when does a six-year-old know the time to the exact minute – without being prompted? And when the Public Prosecutor asked one of the boys how he knew these details, the answer came back: 'Because grandfather told me.'

I knew that my children's statements could not be taken as evidence in a court of law because of their young age. But I was aware that these statements could influence the presiding judge, and that the defence lawyers would use my children's statements as much as they could. And so, although it hurt me very much to do so, I rehearsed my children's statements until I was completely familiar with every word and able to react to their words in an objective and constructive way.

In the days before my own case was due to be heard I also went to the criminal court, and sat in the court room where my former father-in-law was due to appear. The court buildings were very beautiful, with a sober and solemn atmosphere. The court itself was very formal, with rows of benches facing the judges' bench.

Two judges, together with a public prosecutor, were presiding over the court and on the wall above their heads was the Koranic inscription 'Judge between the people fairly and with justice'. To the left-hand side of the court was a large cage where the accused are held during proceedings. I was told that the judge who would preside over my case was Gamal Abdel-Halim, a man with a reputation for firm sentencing of criminals. I also learned that he was Professor of English in Cairo and that I may be allowed to speak to him in English.

That day in court several men received long prison sentences. Four other men were acquitted, much to the joy of their mothers who shrilled the traditional ululating sound of celebration. Judge Gamal Abdel-Halim immediately ordered that the mothers be removed from the court: nothing was allowed to interrupt the formality of his courtroom.

I also felt it was important to prepare myself for the traumatic occasion of the trial by being as fit and relaxed as possible. I had been on a knife edge for far too long, always close to tears – although not necessarily sad – and I knew that if I didn't take care of myself, there was a danger that I would snap. I decided to take a short break in a delightful place that I had spotted on previous trips to Egypt called Shamoussa Village. It was next to the Bitter Lakes in Fayed, about an hour's drive from Cairo.

I hired a taxi to take me to Fayed, and as we crossed the picturesque bridge I looked along a small river flanked by palm trees. Buffaloes and cows grazed near the water's edge and beautiful birds sang and swooped above them. Shamoussa Village was a magical place, its beach graced with a peaceful beauty which promised to restore my serenity. I stayed in a simple, clean room with a balcony overlooking the Bitter Lakes, and in the distance I could see ships queuing up to enter the Suez Canal.

I ate wonderful food and sat absorbing the sunshine and fresh air, feeling the crippling tensions of the past year melting from me. At night I swam like a porpoise in the safe, warm waters of the lakes, and floated on my back to see more clearly the moon that lit the lake almost as brightly as the sun had done by day. I slept totally intoxicated with Egypt and woke at 3.30 a.m. to a scene that no artist could imitate. I hardly wanted to draw breath for fear of disturbing the air around me. I saw a small fishing boat on the lake with two fishermen drawing their nets in the most beautiful sunrise that I have ever seen.

I had experienced inestimable loss and violence in Egypt, but I had also experienced great kindness, warmth and support. I remembered how, after the stabbing, the hospital switchboard had been jammed with messages from well-wishers, anxious to assure me that Egyptians everywhere were on my side. And now I was drawing further strength from the rejuvenating power of Egypt's magical landscape.

I returned to Cairo feeling regenerated, with my confidence restored, ready to face the ordeal of the trial. On the night before the trial, I prayed fervently to God for justice the next day. And in my sleep I dreamed that my father was with me. I could feel his arms around me as I slept in total peace, and my father was saying to me, 'You'll be all right, darling.' The next morning as I sat in front of my dressing table putting on my make-up, I marvelled at how utterly relaxed I felt in the face of the traumatic experience I was about to face.

Suddenly, I remembered my dream, but I felt that it was more than a dream: I was sure that my father had somehow come to comfort me, and I was sure that his presence was still with me. I sat for a while, thinking of my father, and thanking God. I finished dressing and went downstairs, ready to make the short journey to court, and every step of the way I felt that my father was walking with me.

The British Pro-Consul had told me that, in Egypt, victims of violence and even judges had been attacked by the angry families of criminals after strong sentences had been served on them. He had advised me to protect myself from such an attack by going to the Chief of Security at Heliopolos Criminal Court as soon as I arrived there. The Chief of Security couldn't have been more helpful and four armed guards were assigned to protect me in the course of the trial.

I went to sit on a bench outside the courtroom, feeling quite relaxed and waiting for the session to begin. Then, to my horror, I heard the grandfather's booming voice asking me to shake his hand – the same hand that had nearly knifed me to death one year before. I didn't take my eyes off that hand as I shouted for help. Guards rushed to my side and the grandfather was handcuffed and taken away to the cells below the court building. (Those facing serious criminal charges are supposed to be taken straight from their cells into the courtroom cage, but somehow the grandfather had been taken through the public area of the court.)

My relaxed state of mind had been destroyed, but Madeh Ahmed came to my aid with words of comfort and much-needed coffee. I was doubly glad that she was sitting with me when I saw Abdel-Salam's brother Gamal and two of his uncles from Sukaria come up the stairs to sit directly opposite me, staring maliciously. I stared back without flinching, and in the end, it was they who turned their eyes from mine.

When they got up and went into the courtroom I followed, and there, in the prison cage, was the grandfather. He was smoking a cigarette, looking insolent and trying to pretend that he was unconcerned about the proceedings. I crossed the courtroom and sat down right next to him, only the thick wire of the cage separating us. I wanted to be able to look directly at the grandfather, showing him that I was not afraid of him and adding to his discomfiture. But soon Madeh came and spoke in a gentle whisper to me: she asked me to sit with her so that we could be ready when our case began.

I was feeling confident and well versed in the format of criminal proceedings, thanks to my lengthy consultations with Madeh. I knew that my case was a public prosecution, which meant that charges were being pressed against the grandfather by the Egyptian government, rather than by me as an individual. I also knew that the lawyer for the defence would be the first to address the judge.

And then I heard our names: 'The Public Prosecution call Mohammed Abdel-Salam El-Sawy and Hebba t-Allah Ahmed.' The case had started. I glanced behind me to the very back bench where I knew that Gamal was sitting with his uncles. His head was in his hands, and I couldn't help feeling glad to witness his suffering. His mother – together with the other women of the family – had stayed at home.

I turned back to face the judges' bench and listened carefully to all that was said. As the seriousness of the charges against Mohammed El-Sawy became apparent to the spectators in the court, the atmosphere in the court-room changed perceptibly, becoming intensely dramatic.

And as I heard the grandfather's lawyer put forward his defence, I knew that their case was extremely flimsy: 'This woman arrived in the middle of darkness at dawn,' he claimed, 'and kidnapped my client's granddaughter. Not satisfied with that, she tried to kidnap his two grandsons too. She had with her five men whom she had paid to help commit this crime, and they were all carrying knives. We commend Mohammed El-Sawy for protecting his grandchildren.'

He literally spat out his next words: 'This woman held my client from behind, her arm around his neck, and as the five criminals that she had paid tried to stab a grandfather protecting his grandchildren, one of the knives accidentally penetrated her body.'

This was all that the defence amounted to (my children's 'evidence' was not admissable because of their ages) and the notion that I had overpowered the grandfather was clearly absurd. The grandfather was a big man whereas I am five foot three inches tall and weighed about eight stone at the time.

As soon as the lawyer had spoken, I stood up, knowing that I looked frail and small, and took my jacket off. I saw the judges looking from me to the grandfather and back again – and drawing the obvious conclusion.

Then it was Madeh's turn to put my case. She spoke quietly and with dignity and all eyes turned to Mohammed El-Sawy as Madeh gave a detailed account of his attack upon me. There were gasps of horror from the courtroom. I don't know how I managed to control the waves of nausea that washed over me, but I was determined to stay in control of myself in order to be ready to give my evidence to the judges.

That day as I listened to an objective account of the violence against me, I realized just how much I had blocked out of my mind. It was traumatic to have to relive that experience in court, yet I found that it refuelled my anger and strengthened my resolve to see justice done – and to win my children back. Having faced my own nightmare, I turned to the grandfather and stared him straight in the eyes. What I saw in his eyes frightened me more than anything: there was not the slightest indication of remorse on his face, only a look of blatant arrogance and an unmistakable sneer.

And then Judge Gamal called me, asking me in English to give him my account of that violent day. As I walked towards him, I felt that I had nothing to fear. Meeting his eyes, I saw a kind, fatherly face which invited me to confide in him. I told him all that had happened from the very beginning, including the abduction of my children. I became so involved in what I was saying, that I all but forgot I was in a court of law. I ended by pointing to the grandfather: 'I could forgive this man for everything that he has done to me,' I told the judge, 'if only he would return my children.'

Then I sat down and waited, watched and listened while the judges and the public prosecutor deliberated. Would justice be done? Or would the grandfather – an Egyptian in Egypt – get away with his crime? And then the voice of Judge Gamal boomed out to my former father-in-law: 'Mohammed El-Sawy, where is your son and your grandsons?' The grandfather answered defiantly, 'I don't know, Your Honour.' Judge Gamal asked him three times, and each time he got the same answer.

Then the judge said, 'These are very serious charges against you. I will not pronounce judgement today. Instead, I will give you one more day to try to remember where your son and grandsons are. Try to remember, so that I can be lenient with you.' I left the court that day praying that Mohammed El-Sawy would relent and that my children would be brought to me.

The next day, I went back to court to hear Judge Gamal speak sternly yet again to the grandfather, asking him if he had remembered where my children were. But the grandfather refused to tell. 'One more day, Mohammed El-Sawy!' warned the judge. 'Tomorrow I will sentence you.'

The third day in court was one that I will remember all my life, and I hope one day to be able to tell my grandchildren about it. Judge Gamal had given permission not only to journalists, but to press photographers, to be present in the courtroom when he pronounced sentence, and many of my old friends and allies from the newspapers and from BBC Cairo were present – as well as journalists I had never seen before.

The atmosphere was thick with excitement. Photographs of the judges were taken before the proceedings began while I answered questions outside the courtroom. I was not expecting the grandfather to change his mind at this stage to reveal the whereabouts of my children, but I did feel that this degree of media interest was bound to help us in the longer term.

When Judge Gamal came into the courtroom, a hush descended: the man who had almost murdered me was only minutes away from judgement. I was now very nervous, absorbing every word and every detail of the proceedings through all of my senses. I could smell the fear of the grandfather, the excitement of the media and the anticipation of my lawyer.

But I could not allow myself to anticipate success or failure. I felt very small and helpless and found myself praying to God in Arabic for protection and justice: 'Hasbia Alla, wa ne'ama el-wakeel', repeating the words again and again, knowing it was only minutes before the whole case was over.

I remembered my children's suffering and my own. In my mind's eye I saw Yasmeen, who was staying in England with Kath, and I imagined my sons sitting in an Egyptian school not far away from me. They could not know the significance of this day as they worked and played in their own little worlds. And as though I was watching myself being stabbed on a film, I recalled the violent day on which I had barely escaped death.

And then I heard Judge Gamal speak to the grandfather: 'Mohammed Abdel-Salam El-Sawy, you are a disgrace to your country and a disgrace to the religion of Islam. Egypt disowns you. You denied your grandchildren the warm embrace of their mother, and their mother you denied her motherhood.' Judge Gamal went on heaping disgrace upon the grandfather, first in Arabic and then in English to make certain that I understood.

And then it was my turn to stand before Judge Gamal. It was as if – after fighting alone for a very long time – someone was at last acknowledging my struggle and offering sympathy for the suffering I had been through. I felt so weak at the knees that at one point I had to support myself by holding on to the bench in front of me. Judge Gamal said: 'And about you, Madam Hebba t-Allah. Egypt salutes you for your bravery, strength and courage, and Egypt urges you to continue your fight for your children who are yours by right in Egyptian law.'

I felt that the judge was speaking on behalf of all of Egypt. His words comforted me and gave me solace, wrapping themselves around me like a long-awaited, warm embrace. The lady sitting next to me was in floods of tears. So many emotions were going through me that I could hardly feel them.

Then the courtroom was silent. I held my breath. I felt sick. I closed my eyes and time stood still. My eyes were still closed when I heard Judge Gamal pronounce sentence. His voice was stern and dramatic:

'Mohammed El-Sawy!' He paused.

'Seven years imprisonment!' From the deliberate silence that followed, I knew that there was more to follow.

'Seven years, with hard labour. And £50,000 (Egyptian) compensation to pay!' (This compensation money was never paid to me.)

A victory for me and my children! Suddenly journalists and photographers seemed to flood the courtroom, as cameras flashed and flashed again. I was laughing and crying at the same time, and so were many of the journalists. No more would the grandfather be able to hurt Yasmeen or Sawy or Sammie. I couldn't wait to telephone Yasmeen with the good news. And then it dawned on me that he would not be able to hurt me again either.

But I had unfinished business with my would-be killer. I walked towards the cage and said to him in Arabic: 'Mohammed El-Sawy; you see now that there is justice in Egypt!' And then he was led from the cage by guards to an armed vehicle – and seven years in prison.

Chapter Eighteen

Since the grandfather's trial and imprisonment for attempted murder (he died of a heart attack in prison in April 1993) I have continued to try to get my children back. At intervals I have flown to Cairo, attended court hearings and tried yet again to find a team of reliable men who will rescue my children.

In 1992, I paid £500 to Egyptian army officers who said they would rescue my children. They claimed that they could locate Sammie and Sawy using the state security network, but nothing happened and I never saw the money again.

In between times I have tried to publicize my case as widely as possible, putting pressure on the UK and Egyptian governments alike to take some action.

At the end of 1991, Esther Rantzen's *Hearts of Gold* TV programme awarded me the title of 'Best Mum in the World' after Yasmeen wrote and told them of how I had nearly died trying to rescue her and her brothers. The programme presented me with a brand new car which sadly, I was forced to sell. When I rang to explain this to them their researchers kindly told me, 'Don't worry; we knew you needed cash and that's why we gave you the car . . .'

Also in 1991, a BBC *First Sight* television team took me to Cairo to make a documentary film about my case. The film was shown in the UK in November 1991, only days after the children's grandfather had been imprisoned. It struck me then that this would be a good opportunity to approach the Egyptian owner of Harrods, Mohammed El-Fayad, for help in recovering my children.

I faxed him a message to suggest he watched the documentary, and to my delight Mr El-Fayad's Press Secretary, Michael Cole, rang me the next day. He explained that as a family man Mohammed El-Fayad had been moved by my dilemma, that he had a daughter called Yasmeen of about the same age as my Yasmeen, and that he wanted to help me as much as possible.

At the end of November 1991, Yasmeen and I travelled up to Knightsbridge to meet the famous chairman of Harrods. My hands were clammy with nerves as we were met on the sumptuous fifth floor by Michael Cole, who did his best to make me feel more relaxed.

Mohammed El-Fayad was extremely charismatic, kind, warm and very natural. He chatted with Yasmeen affectionately, tousling her hair and asking her if she would like a nice new party frock for Christmas. He put a Harrods assistant at Yasmeen's disposal and she chose an elegant black velvet cocktail dress with a £400 price tag – far beyond anything that I could have bought her. (The assistant asked Yasmeen, 'Do you believe in Father Christmas?' She replied, 'No, but I believe in Uncle Mohammed!'.)

He also promised me his help in recovering Sammie and Sawy. He told me that he would pay my legal fees and that he would try with his own contacts to locate my sons. He also helped me by putting me in touch with staff in his own travel agency in Cairo, should I ever need help while in Egypt. I am enormously grateful for both the sympathy and the practical and financial help that he gave me.

Before we said goodbye, Mohammed El-Fayad asked me not to think badly of all Egyptians because of my terrible experiences. I replied in Arabic that I loved Egypt and knew better than to judge all Egyptians on the basis of my ex-husband's behaviour.

As Yasmeen and I left Harrods, Mohammed El-Fayad gave me an envelope, told me not to beg in pubs any more and suggested that I come to him for help instead. Yasmeen and I were sitting in the Harrods Tea Room when I opened the envelope. It contained £1,000 in crisp new fifty-pound notes. I burst into tears, not for the first time that day, and Yasmeen said, 'Can we have Kentucky Fried Chicken tonight then Mummy?'

While in Cairo in early 1991, I had heard that President Mubarak of Egypt and his wife Suzanne – a prominent supporter of children's charities and the Egyptian equivalent of Princess Diana – were making a state visit to Britain in July. I decided that I would use their visit to get publicity for my case.

I telephoned the *Daily Mirror* journalist Harry Arnold and he offered to help me by finding a 'window' in the President's visit. He rang back and told me that Madame Mubarak would be visiting the Egyptian Embassy in South Audley Street, central London, on the morning of 24 July. Harry said he would cover my story and bring a photographer. Sky TV and my local paper also agreed to cover it, while Thames TV sent a car and drove Yasmeen and me to the Embassy.

The policeman on duty at the Embassy wouldn't let me through their cordon to the door, but they did tip me the wink when the official car was due to arrive. Carefully judging the moment, I stepped in front of Madame Mubarak as she got out of the official car and – with cameras rolling – I said, 'Please Madame, please help my children.'

I gave her a letter telling her that my sons were being hidden in Egypt, that I had nearly died in one attempt to rescue them and that I needed the support of the Egyptian government to get them back again. On her way into the Embassy, Mrs Mubarak, surrounded by her bodyguards, hardly reacted to my plea. But when she left the Embassy two hours later she smiled at me and made the traditional Egyptian gesture of touching below each eye with her finger to show that she would 'give her eyes' to help me.

Much encouraged, that evening I went to meet a well-connected Egyptian contact who had promised to introduce me to the President's aide and the Egyptian Minister for Information. By the time we met, I had been on national television five times and they had no difficulty in recognizing me.

As I told these senior government officials the details of my case, they reacted with apparent concern and sympathy. When I had finished speaking, the President's aide said to me, 'I promise you Madame Hebba, if I have to imprison every member of your ex-husband's family, I will find your children!'

I wrote to the British Embassy in Cairo telling the Ambassador of this promise, and the Embassy wrote to the government reminding them of what had been said and keeping up the pressure. But nothing happened and I came to believe that the 'promise' was a simple ploy to keep me quiet. As far as I know, neither the President's aide nor Mrs Mubarak ever did anything to help my children.

However, almost a year later in mid-1992 I received a message from General Saad El-Gamal of the Police Department in Cairo. He contacted me through the British

Embassy and offered to arrange an access visit with my children. I was very excited about this, assuming that the General knew where my children were, and I began to make arrangements to go to Cairo.

I was due to go out to Cairo anyway for another court hearing, so I would also see General Saad El-Gamal and, I hoped, Sammie and Sawy. I had high hopes that the General had found my children, but when I went to see him he said, 'Just tell me where they are, and I'll go and get them for you.'

In my disappointment I managed to explain that my ex-husband's family was hiding the children and that I didn't know where they were. The General told me that if I could get a 'search and find' permit, he would use his forces to look for Sammie and Sawy. I spent the next ten days begging and sobbing at the offices of the Public Prosecutor for Egyptian State Security until I got the necessary permit.

General Gamal eventually told me that my children were not in Egypt and that they had travelled to Yugoslavia with their father on 21 January 1990. At the time, I didn't believe him. Investigations by the Foreign Office and by immigration officials in Yugoslavia revealed that my children had never flown to that country. It seemed likely that the General was lying to me in order to convince me that my children were lost for ever, or dead in a war-torn country. No doubt he expected me to give up the fight and go home. I suspect also that his pride would not allow him to say that he simply couldn't find my children. After another unsuccessful court hearing I returned, dispirited, to England and Yasmeen.

And then in February 1994 came the news that I had looked forward to for so long. A faxed message from the Foreign Office told me that – after four years and some twenty-five court hearings – the Egyptian courts had finally awarded me custody of my children. It had also ruled that my ex-husband must pay the full costs of this long and arduous case. My lawyer Madiha Luxour had kept up my battle for child custody in Egyptian courts, even in my absence. I was so delighted that I whooped for joy and embraced a lot of unsuspecting people that day.

Within hours I had spoken to the *Daily Mirror* journalist Harry Arnold, who with photographer Roger Allen, made immediate plans to fly me out to Cairo. It was essential that I get to Egypt quickly, before my ex-husband's family had time to hide the children or take them to another country. Harry and Roger planned to meet up with me in Egypt for a big story about my reunion with the children.

Yasmeen went to stay with a friend, but on the way to school that day she was in tears. When I asked her what was wrong she at first told me that she hadn't done her homework. But then she admitted that she was afraid for me, going back to the streets where I had been stabbed not so long ago. How unfair it is that Yasmeen, who has been so strong and brave throughout these traumatic years, should still have to carry such a painful burden.

As far as I knew (I have contacts in Egypt whom I pay for information) the boys were living in Sukaria, the village south of Cairo where Abdel-Salam grew up. I had been told that they were living with an old woman who was not even a family member. I was hopeful that, with the right team of men and the help of the Egyptian driver who had helped me in the past, I would be able to go to Sukaria, get the boys into a car and take them home. In Cairo I went straight to see my lawyer Madiha Luxour. Madiha confirmed my view that – although I was entitled to ask the Egyptian police to help me recover my children – the safest course would be to locate the boys as soon as possible and get them out of the country.

As ever, taking them out of the country would be fraught with difficulties. The fact that I had custody meant that I had custody within Egypt – which did not necessarily mean that I would be able to take Sammie and Sawy to England. If my ex-husband had taken legal moves to prevent them from leaving the country, we could be stopped at passport control.

As soon as possible I made contact with the informer who had told me that the boys were in Sukaria. He was living in the neighbouring village and he told me that Sammie and Sawy were still there. He couldn't identify the woman they were living with, but they were being visited every three or four days by Abdel-Salam who was apparently working in Cairo. My hopes were rising and it seemed our long ordeal could soon be over, but I knew better than to trust this information until my Egyptian driver had seen the boys with his own eyes.

While Harry and Roger pored over maps and scanned lists of airline departures to make our getaway, I waited for definite news. There was no way that I, or the journalists, could go to that tiny community of mud huts ourselves without alerting family members that something was about to happen. I also needed to have a clear mental picture of where the boys were living – and with whom – before going to get them. I was aware that we could face opposition: Sukaria is a farming village where people have shotguns and it is still the home of many of the men of my husband's family. These men are a nasty lot; they all have shotguns which they use to settle old scores and questions of 'honour' (usually a girl's chastity) between families.

These same men had watched in court as I testified

against the grandfather. They had helped hide my boys over many years. I knew that I would be safer in the company of two British male journalists, but it was a potentially violent situation. I arranged for five men, night-club bouncers in Cairo, to come with me for protection.

Meanwhile, Harry, Roger and I discussed the problems. Would the boys even want to leave Sukaria? After four years – Sammie was now nearly ten, Sawy eleven – would they even understand English any more? I knew enough about other child abduction cases to be aware that my sons would not come easily. I planned to dissolve valium tablets in fruit juice: if necessary I would give the juice to the boys to keep them calm.

And once we had them in our car, where should we go? They would need time to adjust to seeing me again, to get used to the idea of leaving Egypt. Yet we could not afford to lose any time, and a quick departure from the nearest airport seemed to be the safest solution. Cairo had more flights to European destinations than any other Egyptian airport, yet security was likely to be tightest at Cairo.

But these dilemmas could not be resolved until we knew when – and where – we could get the children. At last, after four days, I was told in a brief telephone call from my driver that the boys were in the village. We would rendez-vous at the Nile Hilton – and then go and get the boys.

I went to the Hilton to wait with Harry and Roger. I could hardly believe that my boys were – again – almost within my reach. For so long I had kept thoughts of them out of my conscious mind – although they regularly appeared in my dreams – and now it was time to prepare myself for seeing them again. Would they even know me? Would they be too big to cuddle? Would they be offended if I touched their cheeks?

I regretted not bringing some toys for them and wondered if I might buy them some things in the hotel shop. But some instinct made me wait: over the years I have had so many disappointments. My mind was quite clear, but the strain of the last few days was making itself felt in my body and I was taking paracetamol for the pains in my abdomen.

The waiting seemed to go on for ever and it was dark before my driver arrived. He walked into the hotel and simply shook his head. Bad news. My informant had lied: the boys were not in the village. He had also checked that the boys were not at the other addresses – in Sharabiya and Gezr El-Suez – where the family might have been hiding them. They had disappeared.

I felt quite numb. If the boys weren't in the village, and weren't at any of the possible Cairo addresses, what hope did I have of reclaiming them? If I could not locate Sammie and Sawy, my custody order was not worth the paper it was written on. My boys could be anywhere in the world. Perhaps General Saad El Gamal had been right. Perhaps they had been taken out of Egypt in 1991. If so, where were they? In the Egyptian community in New York? Or in Germany perhaps? Or, heaven help them, in the former Yugoslavia? For a moment, I faced the fact that I might never see my sons again. I might never know if they were alive or dead. They might not even know if I was alive or dead: after all, the last time they had seen me I was being stabbed on the streets of Cairo.

Harry was quick to make a practical suggestion. We would go ourselves to Sukaria first thing in the morning. If there was any trace of the boys we had a chance of finding something out. If not, we would ask questions of the local people.

We set out from Cairo early the next day and drove south for an hour and a half through the fertile Nile delta until we got to Sukaria. The narrow track, used mostly by donkeys and the odd tractor, was so littered with rubbish and dirt that we had to stop at intervals to clear it in order that the car could carry on. Harry and Roger were shocked to see the black liquid which seemed to boil in the ditch that ran beside the road: this was an open drain and sewer also used for washing by local people.

We stopped the car in among the mud huts that made up the village of Sukaria. It was all much as I had remembered it from years before when I had visited as Abdel-Salam's young bride. It had been a shock to discover then that he had been brought up in one of these mud huts: never had I suspected that my own children would share the primitive conditions of his upbringing.

I had been apprehensive about how the local people would receive us, and as we approached I saw how the narrow, rubbish-littered road would make a quick getaway impossible. But we asked to see the 'Sherrif' (or elder) of the village, who greeted us politely and took us to my ex-husband's family's house where we were met by Ibrahim.

Ibrahim is my ex-husband's uncle and the grandfather's brother. He invited us to sit on the old wooden benches outside his mud house. I noticed at once that not one single woman or girl was out of doors. I asked him, 'Where is your wife?' He told me that she was 'not here'. But I was sure that the women had been told to stay inside the house. (Yasmeen later said to me – and I'm sure she is right – 'The women would have told you where the boys are mum.')

After a period of polite chit-chat – about our health, about the approach of Ramadan – I asked Ibrahim, 'Have you seen my sons, or Abdel-Salam, or Gamal?' He said, 'No, they are not here. We have not seen them since your accident.' (This is how most Egyptians refer to my stabbing.) I then gave him news of Yasmeen, stressing that she belonged to the family too, and I said to him: 'If only Abdel-Salam had not taken the children, all this would not have happened. But now the family is broken up, you don't know where they are, and your brother has died.'

He said: 'Yes, and he was innocent of any crime.' I felt like standing up and showing him the scars that his brother had left on my body, but I restrained myself. It was more important to establish some kind of positive contact. I was quite sure that he was lying: of course he knew where his nephews were. Of course he would not have lost touch with them – or my sons. I also knew from the British Embassy that Gamal's wife Sophie had visited the village within the last year.

I also recognized a young man called Yasser whom I had carried about as a toddler in years gone by. I called him over and worked hard to flatter him, telling him that Yasmeen had always wanted to marry him as a little girl and asking him about his life. He told me that he was a student at Cairo University and I gave him my address and promised we would write to him.

As we said goodbye I forced myself to kiss Ibrahim on both cheeks; this man surely knew where my children were but he was not going to tell me. When I kissed Yasser goodbye I caught a twinkle in his eye. Was he scenting that great prize, a UK visa, perhaps? I felt sure that I would hear from him again. We drank down our cups of tea out of politeness, knowing that stomach upsets would follow (they did), and took the long road back to Cairo.

The next morning I left my hotel and took a taxi to the

airport. I kept my eyes shut as we went through the streets of Cairo. I didn't want to see Egypt if my boys were not here. I shut out all the sights which I knew would only bring back terrible, sad memories. At the airport I hurried through the formalities. Only days before I had seen us, in my mind's eye: Sammie, Sawy and I, together at the check-in desk, together in the airport café. I went through passport control – it would have been a moment of high tension – alone. I boarded the plane without them. And as the plane banked over Cairo's teeming streets (if they weren't there, where on earth were they?) my sense of loss was overwhelming.

And I had yet to break the news to Yasmeen.

But that is by no means the end of my story. Ever since my children were taken I have been through times of crushing depression, but as long as I keep fighting, I can still generate further energy to go on. And I have fought too long to give up now. Yasmeen keeps me to my task, berating me if I don't appear on television or in the newspapers for a while. In 1994 I am concentrating on publicizing my story and bringing pressure to bear on the international authorities.

An Australian television documentary is being made about child abduction which includes the story of my children and this could be shown all over the world. I also have hopes that my boys will be registered with the Missing Persons Bureau in Washington DC. If so, they may be pictured – as many missing children are – on the milk cartons delivered to almost every doorstep in America. Perhaps, a teacher or doctor somewhere in the US will one day notice the faces of Sammie and Sawy and say, 'I know those boys!'

The media – national and local – in this country have long

been a marvellous support and help to me in my campaign. Journalists like Jackie McKeown formerly of the *Croydon Advertiser* have been staunch friends and allies throughout. British politicians too have done their level best to help me in the absence of any agreement with Egypt on international child abduction. Douglas Hurd has tried again and again through diplomatic channels to stress to the Egyptian government that my case is in urgent need of their attention.

Sir George Young, a member of the All Party Committee for the Abduction of Children has been a wonderful support in his work with my case and with the charity Reunite. The MPs Ian McCartney and Angela Rumbold (my local MP) have also been extremely helpful. Now it is time for the British Embassy in Cairo to bring pressure to bear on the Egyptian authorities who must have information about the whereabouts of my ex-husband and Sammie and Sawy.

But why has it so far proved impossible – despite the fact that I have left no stone unturned – to get my children back? Perhaps it is *because* I have left no stone unturned? It seems likely that some of the publicity about my case has backfired. My lawyer Madiha Luxour told me in May 1993 that she had heard through the grapevine that my custody case had taken so many years to reach a verdict because of all the negative publicity surrounding my story. It seems that I am to blame for 'cutting down tourism' in Egypt.

Another journalist who came with me to Cairo had described in an English newspaper how 'little children sold hashish on street corners – and their bodies'. This story was faxed to Egypt and I found myself vilified in the Cairo press and cold-shouldered by previously friendly contacts.

On another occasion, during my visit to Cairo with Caroline Davies of the *Evening Standard*, I was threatened with prison by a senior government official for bringing 'bad publicity' to Egypt.

In the filming of the *First Sight* Documentary too, government officials accompanied the film crew to tell them where they could and could not film, banning them from taking pictures in many parts of Sharabiya. But the television crews went back later and filmed without permission, presenting a grim picture of Cairo.

It may be that the Egyptian authorities finally gave me custody in a cynical move to try to fob me off. Nothing had changed in my case, so why change their minds after four years? Perhaps they were cruel enough to give me custody in the full knowledge that my children were no longer in Egypt.

I am sorry if the story of my fight for my children has not reflected well on Egypt. In spite of all that has happened, I respect many of Egypt's people who have given me enormous encouragement and support, particularly at the time of the stabbing.

But most of all, I love my children. Most of all, I am determined to bring them home.

Postscript

It is now four years since my children were stolen from me. Almost half of my Sammie's young life has been spent away from his mum and in stress and torment. For my Sawy it has been one third of his life, and I know without doubt that these have been four years of scarring emotional crisis. For Yasmeen, although she has coped incredibly with appalling circumstances, this time has brought confusion and a heavy load of depression to carry on her young shoulders.

Yasmeen recently wrote this 'diary' page:

Yasmeen's Diary from 1989 to 1992.

Well, it's hard to explain about my life really. It's as though I've been kicked out of my world, my life, whatever you want to call it. I feel like there's someone out there who wants to hurt me, for what reason I don't know.

All I want is a normal life, but if I ever do have one I am afraid that all of what has happened to me will still affect my life in some way.

I feel as if I'm always being pushed away by everyone. And I can't take it any more because it hurts. I feel like nobody wants me, but if I told my mother she would just say that she was stabbed for me. But it wasn't me that stabbed her, was it?

She also wrote this letter to her father, whom she still loves.

218

She calls him 'Dunhill Daddy' because he smokes Dunhill cigarettes.

Dear Dunhill Daddy,

I think you know why I am writing. To ask why you haven't phoned me. I have left my phone number on the answer machine in Gezr El-Suez and I know that some of the family are still living there because a woman answered and said, 'Yasmeen, are you still awake?'

Oh come on, what's wrong with you? Don't you care any more? It was my birthday on the seventh and I turned twelve. I will be thirteen next year, a teenager, it's hard to believe isn't it? It's hard to believe how time flies; I mean it is as if it was only yesterday that I was nine.

Well, I just want to say that I love you and please send my love to Sammie and Sawy from me and Pam.

XXXX
  XXXX
    (Signed) Yasmeen Ahmed

As for myself, I have been staring at the same photographs for four years, but my children don't look like that any more. They have grown taller, their bones have developed in ways that I don't know about. The same bones that were conceived in my womb have altered dramatically in our enforced separateness. I too have altered.

I wonder what my boys remember about me. Do they remember my crossness when they were naughty? Do they even think about me? Perhaps they have come to hate me, thinking that I took Yasmeen but deliberately left them behind? Am I wasting my energy in fighting for them? I remember other abducted British children that I have helped to return to their mothers. One boy was so brainwashed that he spat obscenities at his mother. If my boys were in front of me now, would they too abuse me? Have they learned violence and aggression from their 'carers'?

Would Sawy turn to me as he does in my nightmares and say, 'I've got my own life now, my own friends. I don't want to come home: this is home . . .'?

What am I supposed to do in the emptiness which their absence leaves? I am so grateful that Yasmeen is back with me, and it's not that she's not enough. It is that I have three children and two of them are still obscenely missing.

I wonder if my boys have forgotten the English language. If I spoke to them in English, would they think of me as a foreigner? How far have their captors gone to drive me out of my sons' minds?

It has become a part of me, being the mother of two kidnapped, missing sons. I have adjusted to this as a way of life and I wonder how I would readjust to their presence. It would be so easy if they were to return to me just as they were when they left. But they will be two strangers, won't they?

I still see my sons everywhere I go. I stare at ten- and eleven-year-old boys, trying to imagine Sawy as tall, gangly, adolescent, boisterous. This is not a game that I enjoy playing, it is a nasty black joke that springs upon me without warning.

There is a boy down our alley who laughs in just the same way as my Sawy does. Did? I felt proud of myself for being able to listen to that laugh, haunting me, without falling apart. I thought – how well adjusted I am, how level headed to hear joy even through my despair. But today, that boy's laughter stripped away the fragile shell I have been building around me, and I hurt. All over again I hurt and hurt and hurt.

I love and miss both of my sons more than my best-chosen words could express. Sawy is a very sensitive child and needed my attention more than the others. I am sure that Sam will be coping better than Sawy and Yasmeen confirmed this. She told me that when Sam was beaten by his grandparents in Sharabiya, that he laughed at them defiantly, even though he knew that he would get an even harder beating.

The grandmother lost nine children in infancy and now she wants mine. I'm sure that she thinks of her dead husband as a martyr for saving his grandchildren from life in an infidel country. If they understood anything about God or religion they would not have condoned their son's evil act. I hope she thinks about all that has happened and that she thinks to herself: 'I wish we hadn't kept Pamela's children from her.'

I have daydreams about how I would punish my ex-husband. I know that it wouldn't right the wrongs that have been done, but I can't help it. In my mind's eye I see myself killing him with the same knife that his father used in trying to kill me. In my anger I imagine punishing him, but I know that God would punish me.

In the meantime I punish myself for leaving my sons behind, working too hard to get publicity for my case, refusing to give myself a rest. I tell my story to everyone, knowing that I need support to carry on fighting, but in doing this I am forcing myself to relive every second of the attack on my life and every disappointment that I have suffered.

Or maybe I want to relive it, all the while looking for the flaw that made me come so close to bringing all of my children home – and yet failing?

More than anything now I want my sons to know that

I'm still alive (was Sammie watching as the grandfather plunged his knife into me?), and that I am still fighting hard for them. I can't bear to think that they may believe I didn't want them: that I only wanted their sister. I love them all the same. I want them all here with me.

But reality has to be faced. I have adjusted to a new way of life; surely they have adapted too. I used to live and breathe for the day that my children and I would all be reunited, but it is different now. Now I realize that – as the months and years have passed – I have begun to coach myself to face life without them. For my own mental well-being I have begun to wean myself of them.

I took their photographs down from the wall to take to Cairo with me while I searched for them. The gap that their pictures left on the wall was like a wound at first, but then the wound healed up. I rehung their pictures today and it was like looking at my sons for the first time. I was flooded with pride. I am their mother, and it can't be wrong to reflect on the wonderful memories of our life together.

24/9/93

Dear Children,

I miss you both so much. I worry about you all the time. I worry about your fears: who helps to make it easier for you when you go to the dentist? Yasmeen told me that you had a tooth pulled out without an anaesthetic, Sawy.

I'm so sorry for being cross with you when you were naughty. I love you so much, darlings. Most of all, I'm sorry that I was stupid enough to let you go away from me.

It is 12.50 p.m. now. This time exactly four years ago, we were all sitting in the café at Heathrow, waiting for your flight to be called. You were both playing with wooden gliders which I had bought for you in the airport shop.

You wore smart suits and bright smiles as you threw the wooden planes high up in the air, watching gleefully as they swooped to the ground. We didn't know as we hugged and kissed each other goodbye that it would be our last happy time together for so many years. I'm so sorry, children.

At the end of my garden in Coulsdon is an alleyway that I know you would ride your bikes along like terrors if you were here. Today is a bright, sunny September day; a back-to-school sort of day, an ordinary, routine English day. But ordinary, routine days departed when you did and since then it has been grief and crisis.

One day soon I will find you and get you home some-how. I will never give up.

Appendix:
International Child Abduction

I never dreamed that my children would be abducted, and until they were, I had no idea that so many other mothers (and sometimes fathers) have had their children so cruelly snatched from them. The despair that a parent feels following a child abduction is so great and so deep that it is impossible to describe. The terror and loneliness that children feel after being snatched is equally unimaginable.

Yet this is a tragedy – and a form of child abuse – which is dramatically on the increase. Child snatching by parents to or from England and Wales rose twelve-fold in the five years prior to 1992, according to the Lord Chancellor's Department (the central authority in child abduction cases). In the year leading up to March 1993, over 1,400 children were abducted from the UK. Most of those may never see their left-behind parent again.

This rise in international custody disputes reflects the growing freedom of movement across borders around the world. All too often, estranged parents both feel that it is their right to have their children with them. Yet unless they can agree on where the children should live, their dispute will be heard in the courts of the country to which the children have been taken – and it is these courts which will decide their future.

The UK is a signatory to two international agreements on child abduction, the Hague Convention (on the Civil

Aspects of International Child Abduction) and the European Convention (on the Recognition and Enforcement of Decisions concerning Custody of Children and on Restoration of Custody of Children). While these Conventions cover most of Europe, North America, Australia and New Zealand (the Lord Chancellor's Department can supply a current list), there are no agreements with most other countries of the world.

If a child is snatched to a Convention country with which the UK has an agreement, the chances of that child being recovered are not good. Of the 350 children snatched to Convention countries (between 1986 and 1992), 159 have been returned. But when children are abducted to non-Convention countries, a parent can face extreme difficulties in visiting a child, let alone bringing that child home.

Egypt has not signed the Hague Convention (which is European in origin and based on Christian laws and customs), and it has no other agreement with Britain on child abduction. However, far from condoning child abduction, Islam states that children belong with their mother. And under Egyptian law, daughters under twelve and sons under ten belong with their mothers as long as she is a 'fit' mother and has not remarried – whether she is a Muslim or not. In practice, it is rare for an Egyptian court to rule in favour of the mother, though if the father remarries and a dispute over custody arises, the mother may appeal.

I believe that, in Egypt, not nearly enough emphasis is placed on the rights and welfare of children. They are often treated as if they were their parents' possessions and are rarely consulted about their own wishes. But children don't belong to us, they belong to themselves and are only 'loaned' to us for a short time. Children represent the future and if we don't treat them with the respect they deserve, we face an unhappy future.

Two sides to every story

My story is one of an English mother fighting for the return of her children from a divorced husband in Egypt, but I want to emphasize that child abduction to the UK also happens, leaving behind desperate parents in other countries.

As I lay recovering from my stab wounds in Heliopolis Hospital in Cairo, a woman came to see me. She had worked as a nurse until marrying an Egyptian doctor from a well-to-do family. They had a son who was five years old and they lived a comfortable life in Heliopolis, a wealthy suburb of Cairo.

She said she was visiting me on behalf of the Middle-Eastern Wives Association in order to wish me well, but it soon became clear that she wanted me to help her abduct her son. She told me how much she missed London and how she had 'gone off' her husband. She wanted to fly to Britain, taking Hussein with her, but she was afraid of being apprehended at Cairo airport as she tried to leave. (This was in spite of the fact that when her husband proposed to her, he had warned her that he had no intention of living anywhere other than Egypt – and that she should take that carefully into account before accepting his proposal.)

I was offended that she should ask me to help her abduct her son, just days after I had been stabbed while trying to rescue my own children from abduction. There was in fact nothing to stop her from leaving Egypt, and she did abduct Hussein to London. I have since met her husband, a sad and desolate man who deeply feels the loss of Hussein, and I have offered to help him gain access. I sought legal advice and discovered that Hussein would almost certainly be returned to Egypt by a British court order if the father petitioned the courts in this country.

The irony and injustice of this situation – as contrasted with my own – is enough to make anyone feel bitter. British courts will agree to reinstate children to the country of their birth – yet they seem powerless to bring British-born children home. My own British court order for custody was totally disregarded in Egypt. Britain could surely do more to make sure that the children of its own citizens are protected.

What can be done?

In March 1993, the Parliamentary All Party Group on Child Abduction published its report 'Home and Away – Child Abduction in the 90s'. The report was the culmination of two years' investigation by the All Party Group, together with the charity Reunite, parents and other interested professionals.

Their chief recommendations included:

● More careful checks on people travelling with children to non-Convention countries (or countries with poor records for implementation of Convention agreements)

● Investigating the usefulness of passports for children

● Government initiatives to encourage more countries to sign the Hague and European Conventions

● A Children's Ombudsman to be appointed at the Foreign Office

- Government funding for the voluntary sector which currently does the work of preventing abductions and recovering children

- Education for the professionals (police, immigrations officials, legal professionals and social workers) on the issues of child abduction

- Harmonizing the legal system within Britain so that judgements and Legal Aid certificates are enforceable across the UK

- Government funding for mediation services, contact centres and court cases concerning child abduction

As things stand, not enough is being done to stem the fast-escalating problem of international child abduction. Perhaps it is too late for my own tragedy to be turned into a story with a happy ending, but one of my great hopes is that this book will raise public awareness, both in Britain and in the rest of the world. Perhaps stories like mine will nudge heads of state towards the negotiating table where they can begin to talk about the tiny forgotten hostages of international child abduction.

Resources

REUNITE

Reunite, the National Council for Abducted Children, is a charitable organization founded in 1987 to give advice, information and support to parents of abducted children. It aims to advise on how to recover children who have been abducted, and to prevent child abduction from occurring in the first place. Reunite is asked to help parents and professionals all over the world and has been involved in cases in over fifty countries.

Reunite offers a volunteer-run counselling service so that parents who contact the organization can talk to another parent who has been through a similar experience. Reunite also brings together parents whose children have been abducted to the same country so that they can share their knowledge and offer mutual support.

Reunite offers advice and information on:

- national and international law

- English-speaking lawyers at home and overseas with experience of child abduction work

- non-statutory child abduction organizations overseas

- how to raise money

Write to:

Reunite
National Council for Abducted Children, PO Box 4,
London WC1X 3DZ. Tel: 071 404 8356.

Other useful telephone numbers and addresses

The Child Abduction Unit
The Lord Chancellor's Department, Trevelyan House,
30 Great Peter Street, London SW1P 2BY
Tel: 071 210 8500 (switchboard), 071 210 8704/8746/8530
(direct lines).

Foreign and Commonwealth Office
Consular Department, Clive House, Petty France
London SW1H 9HD. Tel: 071 271 8629.

The United Kingdom Passport Agency
Clive House, Petty France, London SW1H 9HD.
Tel: 071 271 8629.

Other information and assistance can be provided by

Your local Citizen's Advice Bureau

Your local police station (which may be able to check
through the police in the country to which the child has
been taken that the child is safe and well).

Telephone numbers of the nearest CAB and police station
are listed in local telephone directories.